Buddhist Wisdom Books

BY EDWARD CONZE

BUDDHIST MEDITATION
BUDDHIST THOUGHT IN INDIA

The frontispiece of the Tun Huang Print of the *Diamond Sutra*, A.D. 868, now in the British Museum.

Buddhist
Wisdom Books

CONTAINING

The Diamond Sutra

AND

The Heart Sutra

Translated and explained

by

EDWARD CONZE

London
GEORGE ALLEN & UNWIN
Boston   Sydney

First published in 1958
Second edition 1975
Second impression 1980

GEORGE ALLEN & UNWIN LTD
40 Museum Street, London WC1A 1LU

© George Allen and Unwin Ltd., 1958, 1975

ISBN 0 04 294090 7

Printed in Great Britain in 11pt. Old Style type
By Billing & Sons Ltd, Guildford, London and Worcester

Preface

There was a time when wisdom was prized more highly than almost anything else, and it was no mean compliment when the Delphic oracle named Socrates as the wisest of all the Greeks. Nowadays most people will agree with Bertrand Russell 'that, although our age far surpasses all previous ages in knowledge, there has been no correlative increase in wisdom'. At times it may even appear as though the rapid growth of scientific knowledge has been bought at the expense of much of the wisdom which our less well-instructed forefathers could draw upon. If literary documents are anything to go by, past ages had a better record than our own, and we have nothing to show that could rival the ancient wisdom literature of Greece and India.

In fact, those who want to learn about wisdom, must of necessity draw on the tradition of the fairly remote past. For centuries almost everyone has been silent on the subject. Philosophers, of whom some 'love of wisdom' might be expected, have increasingly turned to the critical examination of knowledge, and are largely engaged in active disparagement of all that once passed for 'wisdom'. Nor has the effect of scientific and technical progress been any more propitious. What, indeed, could be more 'unscientific' than the pursuit of wisdom—with its concern for the meaning of life, with its search for ends, purposes and values worthy of being pursued, with its desire to penetrate beyond the appearance of things to their true reality? In a world occupied with the manipulation of sense-data the contemplation of suprasensory essences seems an almost grotesque undertaking. Contemporary religious movements are equally unhelpful. Intent on extreme simplification, they take pride in discarding the intellectual content of religion. Whether we look to Billy Graham and Moral Rearmament, or, farther East, to Krishnamurti and the Shin-shu of Japan, the demands made on our intellect and comprehension are reduced to a minimum.

By contrast, two thousand years ago both the Mediterranean and India went through a particularly creative period, which saw the Hebrews writing about *Chochma*, the Gnostics about *Sophia*, and the Buddhists about *Prajñāpāramitā*, or 'perfection of wisdom'. In spite of many differences caused by the social and cultural background, the wisdom tradition at that time achieved a fair degree of universality, and its Indian form was distinguished more by its uncompromising sublimity and other-worldliness, than by the peculiarity of its tenets. The works of Proclus and Dionysius Areopagita, and even the *Academica* of Cicero, show that some of the specific teachings of the *Prajñāpāramitā* were once quite familiar to the West.

The *Prajñāpāramitā* literature consists of thirty-eight different books, composed in India between 100 B.C. and A.D. 600.[1] The judgement of thirty generations of Buddhists in China, Japan, Tibet and Mongolia has singled out two of these as the holiest of the holy—the *Diamond Sutra* and the *Heart Sutra*, both perhaps of about the fourth century of our era. The first is known in Sanskrit as the *Vajracchedikā Prajñāpāramitā*, the 'Perfection of Wisdom which cuts like a thunderbolt'. The second sets out to formulate the very 'heart', 'core' or 'essence' of perfect wisdom, and is as diligently studied in the Zen monasteries of Japan as in the lamaseries of Tibet. The authors of these works were well aware that language is ill-suited to expressing the insights of a wisdom which aims at no less than the total extinction of self. For, to quote Plotinus, 'how shall a man behold this ineffable Beauty which remains within, and proceeds not without where the profane may view it?' Nevertheless, the Sages of old have thought it worth while to attempt the impossible, and some good will perhaps come from making their work available to the distracted world of today. Commentaries are not a particularly rewarding form of literature, being neither easy to write nor pleasant to read. But ready intelligibility does not go well with depth of thought, and these texts require a great deal of explanation, which I have supplied from the traditional Indian commentaries. All the terms have been explained, and most of the arguments. What I have left unexplained, seemed to me either obvious or unintelligible.

[1] For a survey of this literature, with copious extracts, see E. Conze, *Selected Sayings from the Perfection of Wisdom*, 1955.

The greater part of this book has first appeared in the pages of the *Middle Way*, the journal of the London Buddhist Society. I am grateful to Mrs M. H. Robins, the editor, for first having printed these articles, and now allowing me to reprint them. The work on these translations and commentaries has occupied me for more than twenty years, and in the course of this time I have had many useful suggestions from friends and fellow-workers. I particularly want to acknowledge the help of Professor F. W. Thomas, Dr E. J. Thomas, Professor T. Burrow, Professor G. Tucci, Miss I. B. Horner, Mr Christmas Humphreys, Dr Eichhorn, Dr F. G. Brook and Mr T. Perkins. I also thank Miss Pat Wilkinson for the skill and devotion with which she has drawn the mantra on the eight-petalled lotus on page 103, which is based on a ninth-century model from Central Asia.

For the *Heart Sutra* I have given the original Sanskrit text, as it emerges from a comparative study of the extant manuscripts, twenty-one in number. Considerations of expense have deterred us from doing the same for the *Diamond Sutra*, and I must refer the reader to my Rome edition which gives all the alternative readings. The English translation of the actual text of the Sutras is printed in **bold type**. My own explanations use ordinary print, but the terms of the Sutras are repeated in **bold type** wherever they are being explained. Generally speaking it would be difficult to find anything as remote from the interests of the present day as the contents of this book. This in itself may recommend it to some of those for whom it is intended.

London   EDWARD CONZE
September 1957

Contents

THE HEART SUTRA
Sanskrit text, translation and commentary

The Diamond Sutra

Introductory Note

The *translation* of this Sutra is made from the Sanskrit text, and based on my Rome edition of the *Vajracchedikā*.[1] The translation here differs from the one printed there (1) in that it does not try to reproduce the peculiarities of the Sanskrit syntax, and uses a slightly more idiomatic English; and (2) that it omits the additions which various scribes have after A.D. 500 now and then inserted into the text.

Indian tradition assumes that without a *commentary* a holy book is incomplete. In the case of the *Diamond Sutra* it is quite obvious that a bare translation cannot possibly convey its full meaning. To the casual reader it must present the disconcerting appearance of a jumble of disjointed pieces, and at first sight the transition from one chapter to the next is not at all obvious. An occasional aphorism here and there may strike his intellect with the force of a thunderbolt, and further meditation may very well fan the initial spark into quite a sizeable flame. But the meaning of the Sutra as a whole is bound to elude him, for it contains within itself only few and inconclusive clues to its logical sequence. Unless he has outside sources of information at his disposal, he will remain mystified, and soon turn to something else.

For the last 120 years the *Diamond Sutra* could be read in European translations, and during all that time we have been without the means which would have enabled us to solve its riddles. All of a sudden the situation has changed, and we now approach the task of interpreting this Sutra with greater confidence than before. No longer need we rely on mere guesswork, or the fading and unsubstantiated memories of what we may have learned in former lives. The admirable enterprise and scholarship of Professor Tucci has now placed three authoritative

[1] Edward Conze, *Vajracchedikā Prajñāpāramitā*, edited and translated with Introduction and Glossary. Rome. Ismeo, 1957. Serie Orientale Roma, no. XIII.

Indian commentaries into our hands. Their authors—Asanga, Vasubandhu, and Kamalaśīla—are reckoned among the best minds of Mahayana Buddhism. Their commentaries occupy the first 170 pages of the *Minor Buddhist Texts, Part I*,[1] which Professor Tucci has brought out in honour of the Buddha Jayanti.

In addition, various sources of information have become available during the last thirty years. Some sections of the *Diamond Sutra* reproduce passages or ideas from the large *Prajñāpāramitā Sutras*,[2] and for these we have the comments of Nagarjuna[3] and Haribhadra.[4] And a correct understanding of the technical terms can now be obtained either from the large *Prajñāpāramitā Sutras* themselves,[5] or from Madhyamika authors, like Candrakīrti,[6] and others.

Eschewing all originality, my comments have aimed at carrying on the tradition of Buddhist exegesis which goes back to the great Buddhist universities in Northern India at the time of the Pala dynasty (A.D. 750-1150), and which has been kept alive in Tibet for the last seven centuries. All that I myself have contributed is the English translation of the Sutra itself, as well as the patience to collect the relevant information from my predecessors, and to adapt it to the language and thought of today.

It cannot be the purpose of a commentary to convey directly to the reader the spiritual experiences which a Sutra describes. These only reveal themselves to persistent meditation. A commentary must be content to explain the words used. As such it has some preliminary usefulness, since without having understood even the words one could not easily know what to meditate about. Where we have to deal with highly condensed and extremely profound Buddhist texts, the meaning of the words can be investigated from four angles. For it is in four particulars that they differ from what we are wont to read in the

---

[1] Rome. Ismeo, 1956. Serie Orientale Roma, no. IX.
[2] These passages are listed in my Rome edition on page 9.
[3] *Mahāprajñāpāramitopadeśa*, trans. E. Lamotte, *Le traité de la grande vertue de sagesse*, I, 1944; II, 1949.
[4] *Abhisamayālaṅkarāloka*, ed. U. Wogihara, 1932-5.
[5] *Aṣṭasāhasrikā prajñāpāramitā-sūtra*, ed. R. Mitra, 1888.—*Pañcaviṃśati-sāhasrikā prajñāpāramitā-sūtra*, ed. N. Dutt, 1934.
[6] *Prasannapadā*, ed. de la Vallée-Poussin, 1903-14.

Daily Mail. They are: (1) Buddhist technical terms, (2) in Sanskrit, (3) used by sages, (4) for the purpose of spiritual emancipation.

1. As *Buddhist technical terms* their meaning is very largely determined by a tradition which has carefully defined its key terms in their mutual relationship. It has been the most important part of my task to work out the traditional significance of the terms used. When we have learned that, the Sutras become as familiar to us as her web to a spider, who knows all the connections, and runs up and down the threads with ease. Whether in addition we will also manage to catch some flies, is of course quite a different matter.

2. Secondly, Sutras are written in *Sanskrit*, a highly rational language, capable of great precision, and amenable to thorough grammatical analysis. Not all languages are equally suited to the adequate expression of abstract ideas. Little of these Sutras would, I fear, survive their translation into cockney or the patois of Liège. Literary English benefits to some extent from the influence of Latin—like Sanskrit a largely artificial language. It is nevertheless occasionally very useful to also consult the Sanskrit original. The meaning of Sanskrit words depends very largely on their verbal roots. When words with the same root are translated into English, the similarity of their derivation is sometimes unavoidably obscured, and the unity of the original argument destroyed.[1]

3. Where thinking reaches a certain level of profundity, we must go beyond even the traditional and the direct etymological to the *ancestral* meaning. This is attached to the Indo-European root, and comparative linguistics provides the clue to its ramifications. It may reveal many of the overtones of such words as *śūnyatā* (see *B* 130-1). Similarly, the full weight of a word like *mantra* is felt when kindred words derived from the root *MN* (i.e. *ma, man* or *men*) are considered. These point to an element of eager desire, of yearning and intensity of purpose, of wooing and courting (Greek *mnaomai* and Old High German *minna*), and to an excitement of mind which is far from cool rationality (*mania* = lunacy, and *mainomai*, to rave). The *man-tis*, or 'sooth-sayer', is also concerned with the more persistent and abiding trends of the mind (*meno, maneo,*

[1] I have illustrated this for the two roots *budh* and *jñā* on pp. 98-9.

mnēmē, and so on). Wisdom will use terms always in such a way that the original meaning is revealed. And men were wise long before they became clever. This linguistic correlate of Jung's collective unconscious is surely worthy of greater attention than it usually receives. One of our greatest experts on linguistics, I. A. Richards, has in his *Meaning of Meaning* spoken of the wealth of meaning inherent in many words. 'No one who uses a dictionary—for other than orthographic reasons—can have escaped the shock of discovering how very far ahead of us our words often are. How subtly they already record distinctions towards which our minds are still groping. If we could read this reflection of our minds aright, we might learn nearly as much about ourselves as we shall ever wish to know.'

And finally there is, of course (4) the *spiritual* meaning, which discloses itself not to erudition but to meditation. From a document like the Nicene Creed these Sutras, and particularly the *Hridaya*, differ in that every word refers to actual practices, and is actually verifiable by anyone who takes the trouble to do so. Spiritual discernment cannot, however, be conveyed by written instructions. It presupposes certain qualities of character, a certain direction of the will, and certain habits of behaviour. Where those are present, the intellectual information will come to life, and flare up into a blaze of light. Where they are not, boredom will result, and everything will appear too difficult. The reader will soon know which category he belongs to.

Translation and Commentary

Homage to the Perfection of Wisdom, the Lovely, the Holy!

Prajñāpāramitā texts normally begin with an invocation to the Perfection of Wisdom, and a few words of explanation can be found on page 77. Then follows, as usually, a description of the scene of the sermon:

I. INTRODUCTION

1a. *The Convocation of the Assembly*

1. Thus have I heard at one time. The Lord dwelt at Srāvastī, in the Jeta Grove, in the garden of Anāthapindika, together with a large gathering of monks, consisting of 1,250 monks, and with many Bodhisattvas, great beings. Early in the morning the Lord dressed, put on his cloak, took his bowl, and entered the great city of Srāvastī to collect alms. When he had eaten and returned from his round, the Lord put away his bowl and cloak, washed his feet, and sat down on the seat arranged for him, crossing his legs, holding his body upright, and mindfully fixing his attention in front of him. Then many monks approached to where the Lord was, saluted his feet with their heads, thrice walked round him to the right, and sat down on one side.

Thus have I heard at one time. This is the traditional opening of a Buddhist Sutra. The 'I' who has 'heard' the Sutra, is understood to be Ānanda, who, at a Council held soon after the Buddha's demise, recited all the texts he had heard in the course of his long attendance on the Buddha. In our case these words have more the character of a literary fiction, since the

Diamond Sutra was composed seven or eight centuries after the days of Ānanda.

Srāvastī, the 'City of Wonders', was the capital of Kośala, the Buddha's homeland. Now the village of Sahet-Mahet, in Northern India, near Nepal, it is said once to have housed 900,000 families. Of the forty-five years of his ministry, the Buddha passed twenty-five in Srāvastī.

The **Jeta Grove** was offered to the Buddha by Anāthapindika, who had first bought it from Jeta, its owner, for the price of its surface laid with gold coins. For the story see *BT* no. 1.

Mindfully fixing his attention in front of him. Preparatory to entering into trance, the Buddha fixes his attention on the breath which is in front of him. He then enters into a trance which is described in the larger Prajñāpāramitā Sutras as the 'king of all *samādhis*', and which miraculously persists throughout the preaching of the Sutra.

1b. Subhuti makes a request

2. At that time the Venerable Subhuti came to that assembly, and sat down. Then he rose from his seat, put his upper robe over one shoulder, placed his right knee on the ground, bent forth his folded hands towards the Lord, and said to the Lord: 'It is wonderful O Lord, it is exceedingly wonderful, O Well-Gone, how much the Bodhisattvas, the great beings, have been helped with the greatest help by the Tathagata, the Arhat, the Fully Enlightened One. It is wonderful, O Lord, how much the Bodhisattvas, the great beings, have been favoured with the highest favour by the Tathagata, the Arhat, the Fully Enlightened One. How then, O Lord, should a son or daughter of good family, who have set out in the Bodhisattva-vehicle, stand, how progress, how control their thoughts?'

After these words the Lord said to the Venerable Subhuti: 'Well said, well said, Subhuti! So it is, Subhuti, so it is, as you say! The Tathagata, Subhuti, has helped the Bodhisattvas, the great beings with the greatest help,

and he has favoured them with the highest favour.
Therefore, Subhuti, listen well, and attentively! I will
teach you how those who have set out in the Bodhisattva-
vehicle should stand, how progress, how control their
thoughts.' 'So be it, O Lord', replied the Venerable Subhuti and listened.

Information about **Subhuti** will be given on page 45.—The
Buddha is **Well-Gone,** because on the holy eightfold path he
has gone to Nirvana.

A **Bodhisattva**—from *bodhi* = enlightenment, and *sattva* =
being, or essence. Someone who is destined to become a Buddha,
but who, in order to help suffering creatures, selflessly post-
pones his entrance into the bliss of Nirvana and his escape
from this world of birth-and-death. Sometimes I have translated 'Bodhi-being' where the context seemed to justify it.

A **great being,** *mahāsattva. Mahā* means 'great', and *sattva*
either 'being' or 'courage'. Nagarjuna gives a number of
reasons why Bodhisattvas are called 'great beings'. It is
because they achieve a great work, stand at the head of a
great many beings, cultivate the great friendliness and the
great compassion, save a great number of beings (as in chapter 3). The Tibetans translate *mahāsattva* as 'great spiritual
hero'. According to the *Acintyasūtra* his aspirations are truly on
a heroic scale. He desires to discipline all beings everywhere,
to serve and honour all the Buddhas everywhere, and to purify
all the Buddha-fields everywhere. He wants to retain firmly in
his mind all the teachings of all the Buddhas, to have a detailed
knowledge of all the Buddha-fields, to comprehend all the
assemblies which anywhere gather around a Buddha, to
plunge into the thought of all beings, to remove their defilements, and to fathom their potentialities.

The **Tathagata, Arhat, Fully Enlightened One**—this is
the official title of a Buddha, and it would be too long to
explain here its meaning in detail. For 'Tathagata' see
chapter 29.

Helped—because thanks to the Tathagata the impediments
which at various times threatened their spiritual development

have had no power to effectively hinder it. **Favoured**—because
they were entrusted with this sublime teaching.

Son of good family—Sanskrit *kulaputra* (*kula* = family,
putra = son). A *kulaputra* possesses either a good spiritual
endowment, or a good social position, or both. The word is
regularly used as a polite form of address, and has no very
precise meaning.

Set out in the Bodhisattva-vehicle,—in these Sutras it is
always assumed that salvation can be won in different ways, or
by different paths. Usually three such 'vehicles' are distinguished
— that of the Arhats, that of the Pratyekabuddhas, that of the
Bodhisattvas.

The question at the end is equivalent to: 'How should perfect
wisdom be practised?' **Stand,** or 'abide', refers to the determination to reach enlightenment, which directs all the actions
of a Bodhisattva; **progress,** to his steady growth in concentration and wisdom; **control thought,** to his ability to keep
distractions away from the calm core of his inward mind.

2. THE BODHISATTVA'S CAREER

Chapters 3 to 5 now deal with the career of a Bodhisattva, its
beginning, middle and end. That career begins with the 'Vow',
which expresses his decision to win enlightenment, not only for
himself, but in the intention of benefiting others (chapter 3).
This is followed by the practice of the six perfections, which
extends over many aeons (chapter 4). The last stage of a
Bodhisattva's journey is finally reached with the attainment of
Buddhahood (chapter 5).

2a. *The Vow of a Bodhisattva*

Chapter 3 describes the Vow of the Bodhisattva from four
points of view: (1) As vast—in so far as it refers to 'all beings';
(2) as supreme—because it leads beings to the supreme goal, to
perfect Nirvana; (3) objectively as absolute—'in reality no
being exists'; (4) subjectively as unperverted—unmarred by
false views about self, beings, and so on. This chapter is taken

from the large *Prajñāpāramitā*, and the earlier version can be consulted in *SS* no. 87.

3. The Lord said: Here, Subhuti, someone who has set out in the vehicle of a Bodhisattva should produce a thought in this manner: 'As many beings as there are in the universe of beings, comprehended under the term "beings"—egg-born, born from a womb, moisture-born, or miraculously born; with or without form; with perception, without perception, and with neither perception nor non-perception,—as far as any conceivable form of beings is conceived: all these I must lead to Nirvana, into that Realm of Nirvana which leaves nothing behind. And yet, although innumerable beings have thus been led to Nirvana, no being at all has been led to Nirvana.' And why? If in a Bodhisattva the notion of a 'being' should take place, he could not be called a 'Bodhi-being'. 'And why? He is not to be called a Bodhi-being, in whom the notion of a self or of a being should take place, or the notion of a living soul or of a person.'

The phrase **should produce a thought** sounds rather clumsy in English. The Sanskrit, i.e. *cittam utpādayitavyam*, alludes to the technical term *cittotpāda*, the 'thought of enlightenment', which marks the beginning of a Bodhisattva's career.

The traditional classification of living beings is a threefold one:

(*a*) By their mode of conception four kinds of organisms are distinguished: (1) Those hatched from **eggs**; (2) those born from a **womb**; (3) those generated from **warm humidity**, such as worms, insects and butterflies; (4) those who are **miraculously born**, and appear all at once, without conception or embryonic growth, with all their limbs fully grown from the very start. Miraculous or apparitional birth is the lot of gods, infernal beings, beings in the intermediary world, and Never-returners. This class is said to be much more numerous than the others.

(*b*) According to whether they are material or immaterial. (1) Material, **with form**, are all living beings, except those which are (2) immaterial, **without form**, i.e. the highest classes of Gods, who correspond to the four formless trances.

(*c*) According to whether they can, or cannot, perceive.

(1) **With perception,** all organisms with sense-organs. (2) **Without perception,** a class of gods, or angels, living in one of the heavens which correspond to the fourth *dhyāna.* (3) **With neither perception nor non-perception,** the very highest immaterial gods, corresponding to the fourth formless *dhyāna.*

The Realm of Nirvana which leaves nothing behind, literally: 'Nirvana without remainder, or substratum.' Buddhist tradition distinguishes two kinds of Nirvana: (1) The Nirvana with substratum, which is attained when all defilements, such as greed, ignorance, etc., are given up. The Buddha reached that at the time of his enlightenment under the Bodhi-tree. But, since he still had a physical body and mental processes, there remained to him the 'substratum' of the five skandhas. This state gave way, at his death, to (2) the Nirvana without substratum. Even the five skandhas disappeared, and Nirvana alone remained. Candrakīrti compares the 'Nirvana without substratum' to a city which, after all the criminal gangs in it have been executed, has now itself been razed to the ground.

2b. *The Practice of the Perfections*

In chapter 4, the perfection of giving is meant to exemplify all the six Perfections, the *Diamond Sutra* being an abbreviated version of the Prajñāpāramitā. The larger works always cover the six perfections in detail. It may even be said, with Vasubandhu, that the perfection of giving includes all the others. The giving of *material things* then represents the perfection of giving in its narrower sense; the giving of *protection* results from the perfections of morality and patience; and the gift of the *Dharma* corresponds to the perfections of vigour, meditation and wisdom.

4. Moreover, Subhuti, a Bodhisattva who gives a gift should not be supported by a thing, nor should he be supported anywhere. When he gives gifts he should not be supported by sight-objects, nor by sounds, smells, tastes, touchables, or mind-objects. For, Subhuti, the Bodhisattva, the great being should give gifts in such a way that he is not supported by the notion of a sign. And why? Because the heap of merit of that Bodhi-being, who unsupported gives a gift, is not easy to measure. What do

you think, Subhuti, is the extent of space in the East easy to measure?—Subhuti replied: No indeed, O Lord.— The Lord asked: In like manner, is it easy to measure the extent of space in the South, West or North, downwards, upwards, in the intermediate directions, in all the ten directions all round?—Subhuti replied: No indeed, O Lord. —The Lord said: Even so the heap of merit of that Bodhi-being who unsupported gives a gift is not easy to measure. That is why, Subhuti, those who have set out in the Bodhisattva-vehicle, should give gifts without being supported by the notion of a sign.

The term **unsupported** recurs at 10c and 14e. It will be explained at 10c.—The word **thing,** also at 14g, translates *vastu*. It means anything associated with the act of giving which departs from a wise attitude to mere emptiness. The larger Sutras speak in this context of the 'Three-fold Purity', i.e. the absence of any thought of giver, gift or recipient. (See *SS* no. 42.)

Notion of a sign: 'Notion' is *samjñā*, also 'perception', 'Sign' (*nimitta*) is a technical term for the object of false perception. It is defined as a thing (*vastu*) which is characterized by the fact that it is imagined, or falsely constructed. A person who 'courses in signs' is someone who takes the data of experience for signs of actually existing realities. The opposite of the 'sign', which is also identified with 'defilement', is the 'Signless', an attribute of the Absolute, which is indeed unrecognizable when met.

The attitude which, in the practice of virtue, ignores all 'things' and 'signs', can be described as completely disinterested. The Bodhisattva is here bidden to forget all about himself, and about the rewards which come to him from his meritorious deeds. The practice of the six perfections must inevitably, in the nature of things, lead to numerous benefits, either in this life or the next. All these benefits—be they honour, prosperity, friends, or good health—are bound up with the **six sense-objects,** collectively known as 'signs'. It would certainly be foolish to despise this quality of 'merit' which is attached to good deeds as their fruit. For **merit** is the indispensable condition for all further spiritual progress. Nevertheless, to aim at merit is to diminish it. **And why?** Because giving, etc., when accompanied by wrong metaphysical views assuming the reality of gift, giver and reward, produces only limited results. But if it aims at emptiness alone, then the reward becomes truly infinite. The selfless Bodhisattva's merit, as Kamalaśila says, is here compared to **space,** or the sky, because it is all-pervading, vast and inexhaustible.

2c. Buddhahood and the thirty-two Marks

Chapter 4 spoke of the 'signs' by which separate things are recognized and marked off. Chapter 5 now deals with the 'marks', by which the body of the Buddha is distinguished from those of other men. As in the world around us we should not look for 'signs' anywhere, so in the Buddha we should not look for the thirty-two marks of the superman.[1]

5. The Lord continued: 'What do you think, Subhuti, can the Tathagata be seen by the possession of his marks?'— Subhuti replied: 'No indeed, O Lord. And why? What has been taught by the Tathagata as the possession of marks, that is truly a no-possession of no-marks.' The Lord said: 'Wherever there is possession of marks, there is fraud, wherever there is no-possession of no-marks there is no fraud. Hence the Tathagata is to be seen from no-marks as marks.'

The **possession of marks** is discussed also at 20b, 26a, 27. The word *sampad*, here translated as 'possession', has other meanings as well, and one might also speak of the 'excellence of his marks', or the 'sum total of his marks'. *Sampad* means the attainments or accomplishments of the individual in the course of his religious career, and the word is regularly used for the 'achievement' of morality, trance, wisdom, or Nirvana.

The connection of the topic of merit with that of the thirty-two marks was immediately obvious to the average Buddhist at the time of the composition of this Sutra. For he was aware that each one of the Buddha's thirty-two marks was born of a hundred acts of merit. He would, however, infer from the

---

[1] Information about these marks can be found in my *Buddhism*, pp. 36–8, and my translation of the *Abhisamayalankara*, pp. 98–102.

argument of chapter 4 that he was wrong in his belief that the six perfections can be practised in the hope of winning Buddha-hood. And this inference is now confirmed by chapter 5. It would, indeed, be a mistake to suppose that Buddhahood is some real, actually existing, condition produced as a result of the merit gained from giving, and the other perfections. It is true that one side of the Buddha, his glorified body adorned with the marks of the superman, is in fact the fruit of this merit. But the real Buddha, in his Dharma-body, is without these marks. In his true reality the Buddha is not produced by anything, and he is also not marked off from anything that would be different from him. It is easy to see that here the Buddha, as he is perceived with the eye of Faith, is contrasted with the Buddha as Wisdom conceives him. And the point of view of wisdom is declared to be the superior and final one.

The term **fraud** alludes to a saying of the Buddha which the Mahayanists were fond of quoting: 'All conditioned things are worthless, unsubstantial, fraudulent, deceptive and unreliable, but only fools are deceived by them.[1] Nirvana alone, the highest reality, is free from deception.' Two classes of facts are here distinguished—the deceptive multiple things on the one side, and the true reality of the Absolute on the other. In its fifth chapter the Sutra prepares the ground for chapters 7 and 26, by pointing out that it would be a mistake to place the Buddha among the false, conditioned things, and that this is done by concentrating on his visible and distinctive features. Our concep-tion of the Buddha must do justice to him as the unconditioned Absolute. It is the constant concern of this Sutra to guard the Absolute against misunderstandings. This theme is so important to it that it recurs again and again, as we shall see in the further course of our exposition.

2d. Buddhahood and the Dharmabody

Chapter 5 contrasted the Buddha's physical body with his essential being. The next three chapters now deal with the Buddha's 'Dharmabody', which is held to represent the absolute reality of Buddhahood. The Dharmabody is considered from

[1] In the Pali Canon a similar statement is made about the sense-pleasures at A.N. V 84, 24–5.

three points of view: (2da) as the body of doctrines, or teachings, in chapter 6; (2db) as the result of gnosis in chapter 7, and (2dc) as the result of merit in chapter 8.

2da. The Dharmabody as the body of teachings

Chapters 4 and 5 expounded a very profound doctrine. They implied a notion of cause and effect which is decidedly peculiar and unusual, in that it had to reckon with the special status of an Absolute which is in itself uncaused and unconditioned. On the other hand, circumstances seem to be rather unpropitious just now for the proclamation of such sublime wisdom. In the present period of history we find ourselves in one of the worst possible cosmic ages, with Buddhism in full decline, and the people everywhere singularly obtuse about matters spiritual, and incredibly dim-witted when confronted with the wisdom of the sages. We may well wonder what point there is in going on trying to teach these things when there seems to be nobody about who can learn them. It is therefore only natural that those entrusted with the Perfection of Wisdom should ask in despair, how anyone in such an age can be expected to believe in this kind of teaching, or to grasp and understand it. The Buddha answers their anxious query by asserting that even now there are Bodhisattvas endowed with the three qualifications necessary to appreciate these doctrines.

6. Subhuti asked: Will there be any beings in the future period, in the last time, in the last epoch, in the last 500 years, at the time of the collapse of the good doctrine who, when these words of the Sutra are being taught, will understand their truth?—The Lord replied: Do not speak thus, Subhuti! Yes, even then there will be such beings. For even at that time, Subhuti, there will be Bodhisattvas who are gifted with good conduct, gifted with virtuous qualities, gifted with wisdom, and who, when these words of the Sutra are being taught, will understand their truth. And these Bodhisattvas, Subhuti, will not be such as have honoured only one single Buddha, nor such as have planted their roots of merit under one single Buddha only. On the contrary, Subhuti, those Bodhisattvas who, when these words of the Sutra are being taught,

will find even one single thought of serene faith, they will
be such as have honoured many hundreds of thousands of
Buddhas, such as have planted their roots of merit under
many hundreds of thousands of Buddhas. Known they
are, Subhuti, to the Tathagata through his Buddha-
cognition, seen they are, Subhuti, by the Tathagata
with his Buddha-eye, fully known they are, Subhuti,
to the Tathagata. And they all, Subhuti, will beget
and acquire an immeasurable and incalculable heap of
merit.

The last five hundred years: It is well known from the
Scriptures of all schools that after the Buddha's Nirvana the
Dharma will progressively decline, and that every 500 years a
decisive change for the worse takes place. The Pali account of
this process can be consulted in *BT* no. 22, and the theory has
been explained in my *Buddhism* (pp. 114–16). 'The last 500
years' are the fifth 500 years, when the Buddhists will be strong
in nothing but fighting and reproving, and the Dharma itself
becomes practically invisible. It is of this period that Vasubandhu says that

> 'The times are come
> When flooded by the rising tide of Ignorance
> Buddha's religion seems to breathe its last!'

Will understand their truth, literally, 'will produce a true
perception', or 'will produce a notion of their truth'. 'True
perceptions' are the prerogative of those 'gifted with wisdom'.
But there is a paradox hidden here: All perceptions are *ipso
facto* false, and a 'true perception', or a perception of what is
really there, is, as we hear in the second part of this chapter,
strictly impossible. In fact it is a miracle, and that is why we
should seek for it.

Next four reasons are listed why these Bodhisattvas are
capable of understanding the meaning of this Sutra:

1. In virtue of their *spiritual accomplishments*, which are of
three kinds, and which 2. they have *deserved* by what they did
in the past. (1a) They are **gifted with good**, moral, **conduct**,
because (2a) they have **honoured the Buddhas** of the past by

doing their bidding, and obeying the moral rules, or precepts. (1b) They are **gifted with virtuous qualities,** because (2b) they have done meritorious deeds in the presence of the Buddhas of the past, and now they reap the reward of the **merit** they **planted** at that time. (1c) They are **gifted with wisdom** in the sense that they have cut off all false notions with regard to persons and dharmas. This is explained in the second half of this chapter, where eight such false notions are enumerated. (2c) The text does not state the kind of behaviour in the past which enables these Bodhisattvas to have so much wisdom at their disposal. From the large Sutras we know that they have for a long time studied the Scriptures with deep faith and great industry (see A, chapter X), and that also they have 'done their duties under the Jinas of the past' (A iii 79). The possession of these three gifts indicates that the Bodhisattvas have been successful in the three kinds of training—in morality, transic concentration and wisdom. The correspondence is not quite obvious for the second item, but we must remember that aptitude for *samādhi* is confined to virtuous people with a sound mental and spiritual constitution built up over many lives.

The times are now so bad that these quite exceptional qualities are needed for even **one single thought of serene faith** in those doctrines. They enable the chosen Bodhisattvas to believe in the Wisdom teachings, and their hearts are gladdened when they hear of them and think about them.

3. In virtue of their being *assisted by the Buddhas.* **Known they are,** etc. This phrase is taken from the large *Prajñāpāramitā.* I quote A x 224, with Haribhadra's comments in brackets: 'It is through the might of the Buddha, through his sustaining power, through his help, that all the Bodhisattvas, the great beings, come to hear of this deep perfection of wisdom, that they bear it in mind, recite and study it, demonstrate, explain, expound, repeat and copy it, and that they progressively train in Thusness. Known they are to the Tathagata (with his heavenly eye), sustained they are by the Tathagata (with his wisdom-eye), seen they are by the Tathagata (with his Dharma-eye), surveyed they are by the Tathagata with his Buddha-eye.' (For an explanation of the 'five eyes' see chapter 18a). And it is of great help to be beheld by the Buddhas. 'The Buddhas will

bring him to mind and assist him. And it is quite impossible to impede anyone who has been brought to mind and upheld by the Buddhas' (*A* x 223).

4. In virtue of the *merit* which they have acquired, and continue to acquire. In our present age, with spirituality observably at a very low ebb, the achievement of enlightenment is normally not feasible. All we can do is to lay the foundations for it at a future period, when conditions will again be more auspicious. 'Merit' is the term for these foundations.

The Sutra next goes on to explain wherein the 'notion of truth' consists, and enumerates eight reasons why the Bodhisatt-vas in question are 'gifted with wisdom'.

And why? Because, Subhuti, in these Bodhisattvas (1) no perception of a self takes place, (2) no perception of a being, (3) no perception of a soul, (4) no perception of a person. Nor do these Bodhisattvas have (5) a perception of a dharma, or (6) a perception of a no-dharma. (7) No perception or (8) non-perception takes place in them.

A wise attitude is here defined by the absence of eight kinds of misconception, or false assumption. The first four refer to mistaken beliefs in some kind of an individual ego, current among Non-Buddhists. The four terms, i.e. 'self', 'being', 'soul' and 'person', have occurred already in chapter 3, and they are nearly synonymous. Buddhist usage distinguishes them as follows: (1) **No perception of a self,** i.e. no belief in the existence of an ego as distinct from the five skandhas, an 'ego' being defined as that of which we could say, 'this is mine, I am this, this is myself'. (2) **No perception of a being,** i.e. no belief in a continuous separate individual identical with himself at different times, who could validly differentiate his internal constituents from what is outside him. (3) **No perception of a soul,** i.e. no belief in the existence of a unifying and vivifying force within an individual organism which, for the span of a life-time, would persist from conception to death. (4) **No perception of a person,** i.e. no belief in the existence of a permanent entity who would migrate from rebirth to rebirth.

The last four items refer to misconceptions about the nature of dharmas, current among Buddhists. (5) **No perception of a**

dharma, i.e. the Bodhisattvas know that dharmas do not exist, and they reject the Abhidharmist conception of a multiplicity of separate dharmas, or ultimate entities. (6) **No perception of a no-dharma,** and that for two reasons: (*a*) The negation of these multiple dharmas opens up one vast emptiness. This 'no-dharma' is more real than the dharmas, but cannot be the object of any possible perception. (*b*) The 'no-dharma' envisaged here is not a simple and clear-cut negation, in that emptiness lies somewhere *between* affirmation and negation, *between* 'is' and 'is not'. Furthermore, these Bodhisattvas have (7) **no perception** at all, because perception normally assigns properties to things, and they know that this arrangement is not founded on fact. They also have (8) **no non-perception,** because they continue to perceive things as other people do, in spite of their knowledge that these perceptions, and the assumptions they take for granted, have no ultimate reality.

And why? If, Subhuti, these Bodhisattvas should have a perception of either a dharma, or a no-dharma, they would thereby seize on a self, a being, a soul, or a person. And why? Because a Bodhisattva should not seize on either a dharma or a no-dharma. Therefore this saying has been taught by the Tathagata with a hidden meaning: 'Those who know the discourse on dharma as like unto a raft, should forsake dharmas, still more so no-dharmas.'

Here we have first of all an allusion to the well-known Mahayana distinction between two stages of the comprehension of 'selflessness' (*nairātmya*). It is not enough to be convinced that there is no 'self' in persons. An impersonal dharma also must be seen as nothing in or by itself, as indistinguishable from any other dharma. The Sutra here claims that the second step is a necessary consequence of the first, and that it alone can prevent a relapse into the 'heresy of individuality'. The reasoning, though subtle, is quite intelligible: No separate dharma can possibly be perceived without a subjective act of **perception** taking place. Now the Abhidharma teaches that the specific function of perception consists in 'taking up' an object, 'noting and recognizing' it, 'seizing upon' it. Similarly, in our own language, 'perception' comes from per-CAP, and *capio* means 'to take hold of, seize, grasp'. But to **seize on** anything, **either a dharma or a no-dharma,** automatically involves an act of preference, bound up with self-interest, self-assertion and self-aggrandizement, and therefore unbecoming to the selfless. As it is said in the *Ashta* (*A* xv 305): 'As contrary to the ways of the whole world has this dharma been demonstrated. It teaches you not to seize upon dharmas, but the world is wont to grasp at anything.'

The reference at the end is to the Simile of the **Raft,** which Mahayanists knew from the Sarvastivadin Scriptures. It also occurs in the Pali Canon, and I quote Woodward's translation from *Majjhima Nikāya:* 'Using the figure of a raft, brethren, will I teach you the Norm, as something to leave behind, not to take with you. If one has crossed with the help of a raft a great stretch of water, on this side full of doubts and fears, on the further side safe and free from fears, one would then not take it on one's shoulders and carry it with one. But though it was of great use to him, he would leave it behind, and have finished with it. Thus, brethren, understanding the figure of the raft, we must leave righteous ways behind, not to speak of unrighteous ways.'

With a hidden meaning: On the face of it, the word 'dharmas' in this saying of the Buddha means 'virtues', and so have Buddhaghosa, Woodward and I. B. Horner (*BT* no. 77) understood it. By taking 'dharmas' not as a moral, but as a metaphysical term, meaning 'entities', our Sutra here discloses the 'hidden meaning' of the simile. This method of interpretation assumes that the Buddha, endowed with supreme skill in means, often chose expressions which could mean one thing for the less, and another for the more advanced, thus proving helpful to both.

The example of the Raft shows that dharmas should be treated as provisional, as means to an end. The same holds good of 'emptiness', the negation of dharmas. This corollary has elsewhere been illustrated by the simile of 'the medicine Agada, which can heal any illness. Once a cure has been effected, it must be abandoned together with the illness, because its further use would only make one ill again. Just so when this medicine, called "emptiness", has brought about a cure of the disease of the belief in existence. Attachment to emptiness is a disease as much as attachment to existence. Those who continue to use this medicine of "emptiness" after they have gained possession of full wisdom, only make themselves ill again' (T 159, 328c).

2db. The Dharmabody as the result of Gnosis

7. The Lord asked: What do you think, Subhuti, is there any dharma which the Tathagata has fully known as 'the utmost, right and perfect enlightenment', or is there any dharma which the Tathagata has demonstrated?— Subhuti replied: No, not as I understand what the Lord has said. And why? This dharma which the Tathagata has fully known or demonstrated—it cannot be grasped, it cannot be talked about, it is neither a dharma nor a no-dharma. And why? Because an Absolute exalts the Holy Persons.

Mahayanists are fond of saying that the Buddha's enlightenment is not a real fact, and that likewise the Dharma preached by the Buddha should not be misunderstood as a definite teaching of definite facts. In the large *Prajñāpāramitā Sutras* the theme of this chapter has been treated at much greater length. A few parallels from the 'Version in 8,000 Lines' may throw light on it, and show the connection with the basic doctrines of (1) the marklessness of all things, of (2) their emptiness, and (3) of their Suchness.

(1) At *A* viii 192 Subhuti asks: 'All dharmas have therefore really not been fully known by the Tathagata?' The Lord replies: 'It is just through their own essential nature that those dharmas are not something definite. Their true nature is a no-nature, and their no-nature is their true nature; for all dharmas have one mark only, i.e. no mark. It is for this reason that all dharmas have really not been fully known by the Tathagata. For there are not two natures of dharma, but just one single is the nature of all dharmas. And the true nature of all dharmas is a no-nature, and their no-nature is their true nature. It is thus that all points of possible attachment are abandoned.' (2) As for emptiness, we have *A* xvi 313–14. Subhuti asks: 'How can the Lord say that full enlightenment is hard to win, exceedingly hard to win, when there is no one who can possibly win it? For, owing to the

emptiness of all dharmas, no dharma exists that would be capable of winning enlightenment. If all dharmas are empty, then also that dharma cannot exist which, as a result of the demonstration of Dharma, we are meant to forsake. And also that dharma which would, or should, be enlightened in full enlightenment, and that which would, or should, cognize (the utmost reality)—all these dharmas are empty. In this manner I am inclined to think that full enlightenment is easy to win, not hard to win.' The Lord replies: 'Full enlightenment is indeed hard to win, because (for lack of a cause) it cannot possibly come about, because in reality it cannot take place, because it offers no foothold to discrimination, and because it does not lend itself to the fabrication of fictitious appearances.' (3) The connection with Suchness is explained at *A* xxvii 453, where Subhuti asks: 'If, O Lord, outside Suchness no separate dharma can be apprehended, then what is that dharma that will stand firmly in Suchness, or that will know this full enlightenment, or that will demonstrate this dharma?' And the Lord replies: 'Outside Suchness no separate dharma can be apprehended, that could stand firmly in Suchness. The very Suchness, to begin with, cannot be apprehended, how much less that which can stand firmly in it. Suchness does not know full enlightenment and on the dharmic plane no one can be found who has either known full enlightenment, will know it, or does know it. Suchness does not demonstrate dharma, and on the dharmic plane no one can be found who could demonstrate it.' These three quotations should suffice to make the teaching perfectly clear.

This dharma, i.e. the ultimate reality, in both its objective and subjective form, **cannot be grasped,** i.e. at the time when it is heard one cannot seize upon it as either a dharma or a no-dharma. **It cannot be talked about,** i.e. at the time when it is preached, one must remain aware that the talk aims at something so high and transcendental that words cannot ever reach it. **It is not a dharma,** not a separate thing accessible to discriminative thought. It is **not a no-dharma,** it is not the negation of a dharma. Psychologically, a negation gives sense only when warding off an attempted affirmation. Where there is no temptation to make positive statements, negations likewise lose their meaning. In other words, dharmas, as strictly empty, cannot even be denied.

The last sentence of the chapter fittingly concludes this argument by indicating the conclusive reason behind it, i.e. the fact that 'this Dharma which the Tathagata has fully known and demonstrated' is the ultimate and unconditioned reality. **Because an Absolute exalts the Holy Persons.** The Sanskrit defies translation, and reads: *asaṃskṛtaprabhāvitā hy āryapudgalā*.

The Holy Persons are traditionally eight, i.e. Streamwinners, Once-Returners, Never-Returners and Arhats (see chapter 9), each one considered either at the moment of entering on his 'Path', or at that of reaping his 'Fruit'. They are called 'holy' in contradistinction to the 'foolish common people', about whom more will be heard at chapter 25 and 30b. Buddhist tradition, in fact, distinguishes two classes of people, the 'common worldlings' and the 'saints' (*ārya*), who occupy two distinct planes of existence, respectively known as the 'worldly' and the 'supramundane'. The saints alone are truly alive, while the worldlings just vegetate along in a sort of dull and aimless bewilderment. Not content with being born in the normal way, the saints have undergone a spiritual rebirth, which is technically known as the 'winning of the Path'. In other words, they have detached themselves from conditioned things to such an extent that they can now effectively turn to the Path which leads to Nirvana. Only they can really be said to 'tread the path' in any proper sense of the term. The worldling's vision of Nirvana is obstructed by the things of the world which he takes far too seriously. Through prolonged meditation he can, however, reach a state where, each time a worldly object rises up in front of him, he rejects it wholeheartedly as a mere hindrance or nuisance. Once this aversion has become an ingrained habit, he can at last take Nirvana, the unconditioned, for his object, 'he ceases to belong to the common people', and 'becomes one of the family of the Aryans'. So Buddhaghosa, who explains the situation in great detail and with admirable lucidity in chapters 21 and 22 of his *Path of Purification*. Thereafter the disciple is less and less impelled by the motives of ordinary people like us, i.e. by motives which are a compound of self-interest and a misguided belief in the reality of sensory things, and which contain a strong dosage of greed, hate and delusion. The contrast with the vision of Nirvana reveals the insignificance and triviality of all these worldly concerns, and Nirvana itself increasingly becomes the motivating force behind whatever is done. In this way the Unconditioned seems to become a kind of condition, the essentially Inactive seems to do something, and that which is nowhere seems to become localized in a definite individual.

The Absolute is literally 'the Unconditioned', and according to Vasubandhu, it means here that which cannot be discriminated. With an obvious and deliberate disregard for logic the Sutra claims that this unrelated Absolute can enter into a relation with certain persons. This is a difficult idea, and a difficult word is chosen to express it. **Exalts**—the word *prabhāvita* contains a great wealth of meanings, and 'exalts' is the best I can do. One could also say, 'are glorified by', 'draw their strength from', 'owe their distinction to', or 'derive their dignity from'. The idea is that the holy persons have 'arisen' from the Unconditioned, have been 'produced' from it, are 'brought forth' by it. It is as a result of their contact with the Unconditioned that they become mighty and powerful, that they 'thrive'. It is by means of the Unconditioned that they 'prevail' and 'excel'. And finally, they are 'recognized', 'characterized', or 'defined' by it, in a sense they are 'revealed' by it. It is their true nature to be the Unconditioned, and that idea is further developed in chapter 9.

2dc. The Dharmabody as the result of Merit

The Dharma, it is true, cannot be grasped or taught, it is neither an entity nor a non-entity. Nevertheless, as productive of merit, the hearing and teaching of that Dharma is not useless.

8. The Lord then asked: What do you think, Subhuti, if a son or daughter of good family had filled this world system of 1,000 million worlds with the seven precious things, and then gave it as a gift to the Tathagatas, Arhats, Fully Enlightened Ones, would they on the strength of that beget a great heap of merit?—Subhuti replied: Great, O Lord, great, O Well-Gone, would that heap of merit be! And why? Because the Tathagata spoke of the 'heap of merit' as a non-heap. That is how the Tathagata speaks of 'heap of merit'.—The Lord said:

But if someone else were to take from this discourse on dharma but one stanza of four lines, and would demonstrate and illuminate it in full detail to others, then he would on the strength of that beget a still greater heap of merit, immeasurable and incalculable. And why? Because from it has issued the utmost, right and perfect enlightenment of the Tathagatas, Arhats, Fully Enlightened Ones, and from it have issued the Buddhas, the Lords. And why? For the Tathagata has taught that the dharmas special to the Buddhas are just not a Buddha's special dharmas. That is why they are called 'the dharmas special to the Buddhas'.

The world system of 1,000 million worlds—this corresponds roughly to what we would call a 'galactic system'. Buddhist scholastics distinguish three kinds of universe according to their size: (1) A universe which comprises 1,000 suns, 1,000 moons, 1,000 Jambudvipa continents, 1,000 heavens, 1,000 hells, etc. (2) A universe which contains 1,000 worlds of the first type. (3) A still larger unit, envisaged here, which combines 1,000 worlds of the second type.

The merit to be derived from giving depends, among other things on the preciousness of the gift, and the quality of the recipient. The gift consists of **the seven precious things,** mentioned also at chapter 11, 19, 28, 32a. They are: gold, silver, lapis-lazuli, coral, gems, diamonds and pearls. When this most precious of all material gifts is given in abundance **to the Tathagatas,** who are the most exalted persons of all, then this act of giving produces a quite exceptional amount of merit. This sounds strange to modern ears. The Tathagatas have all they need, they certainly can make no use of all this gold, silver, etc., and so how could this gift benefit them? Would it not be very much more to the point to relieve the sufferings of those who are in want, and to give them what they need, and what they would use so gladly? Is there not a complete and callous disregard of the poor in the Buddhist statement that the best gift is that which is given by the dispassionate to the dispassionate? Common sense as we understand it must withhold its approval from this statement. Some meditation on the subject is perhaps called for, and it will be all the more fruitful when preceded and accompanied by actual acts of generosity.

Heap of merit—merit is that which either guarantees a happier and more comfortable life in the future, or, alternatively, increases the scope of spiritual opportunities and achievements. One speaks of a 'heap' (*skandha*), a 'stock' or 'store', of merit because the merit which people have acquired in the course of many lives is popularly regarded as a kind of accumulation on which they can draw for various purposes. In fact, however, this heap is really **no heap,** because all its constituents are just empty, and there is no really existing bond which unites them into 'one heap' belonging to anyone.

The merit derived from material gifts is called **great,** that derived from the spiritual gift of the Dharma **immeasurable and incalculable,** 'inconceivable, incomparable and measureless', as *A* iii 71 adds. To be generous with material things brings a 'great' reward—wealth or reputation in a future life, or even rebirth in heaven. Infinitely greater is the reward of those who teach the Dharma. Their spiritual welfare and stature will grow by leaps and bounds, and ultimately they will become fit to gain the Dharmabody of a fully enlightened Buddha.

For the peculiar importance of **this discourse on dharma,** i.e. of the Perfection of Wisdom, lies in that it is the root cause of the enlightenment of the Buddhas, of their very state of Buddhahood. **From it have issued,** etc. This again is a sentence repeated often in the large Prajñāpāramitā Sutras. I quote *A* xii 254–5: 'The Perfection of Wisdom is the mother and genetrix of the Tathagatas. From her they have come forth. For it is she who has shown them that cognition of the all-knowing. From her the all-knowledge of the Tathagatas has come forth. All the Tathagatas, past, future and present, win their full enlightenment thanks to this very Perfection of Wisdom.' And the perfection of wisdom is both the cause and the effect of Buddhahood. 'From her has come forth the state of all-knowledge of the Buddhas', because, when they were Bodhisattvas, the study of the *Prajñāpāramitā* has enabled them to win Buddhahood. 'Conversely, the perfection of wisdom has been brought about as something that has come forth from the cognition of the all-knowing' (*A* x 210–11), because the

Buddhas reveal it to those who are capable of hearing it. In fact, it is possible to say that the Perfection of Wisdom '*is* the true and real body of the Tathagatas. As the Lord has said, "The Dharmabodies are the Buddhas, the Lords. You should not, however, O monks, mistake this individual body for my Body! You should, O monks, see me from the accomplishment of the Dharmabody!" But that Tathagata-body should be seen as brought about by the Perfection of Wisdom' (*A* iv 94). The perfection of wisdom, and the merit derived from teaching it, are therefore here proclaimed as the 'real decisive cause and condition' (*A* iv 95) of Buddhahood. But a qualification is necessary wherever the Unconditioned is apparently being subjected to conditions, as we see from the sequel.

The dharmas special to the Buddhas: The Sanskrit word 'Buddhadharmas' may either refer simply to the attributes which the Buddhas alone possess, or to the well-known list of the eighteen special characteristics of a Buddha (see *BT* no. 140), or to the constituents of the Dharmabody. They are, when ultimate truth is considered, not really properties attributable to a Buddha. In the Absolute there can be no distinction between subject and attribute, between the Buddha and his dharmas, and in consequence they are **not a Buddha's dharmas.** They are also not **special** to the Buddhas, but common to all things, as we are told later on, in chapter 17*d*. The Buddhadharmas lie beyond the categories of reflective thought, and each one must realize them in himself.

In chapters 6 to 8 the consideration of the Dharmabody has led us to the very summit of existence. Up there the air is rather rarified, and we were bound to feel somewhat dizzy at times. The Himalayas of the soul demand no less of us than Mount Everest or Kangchenjunga.

3. THE RANGE OF THE SPIRITUAL LIFE

So far about the first eight chapters. In chapters 9 to 12, the orchestra plays the same tune once again, but with some variations and in a different key. The Sutra first considers (3*a*) the four great, or main, Saints of the Hinayana (chapter 9), and after that the Mahayanistic Bodhisattva first (3*b*) at the

beginning of his career (chapter 10a), then (3c) near its end
(chapter 10b), and finally (3d) at its very end (chapter 10c).
This again, as in chapters 6 to 8, leads us to the Dharmabody
(chapter 10c), and to the merit with which that is bound up
(chapter 11, 12).

3a. The four Great Saints

Chapter 7 already referred to 'the saintly persons', and
claimed that they have all gone beyond karmic coefficients and
the distinctions of conditioned life. Elsewhere, however, the
Scriptures tell us that Streamwinners, etc., obtain a distinctive
fruit of their conduct. How can this contradiction be resolved?
The answer lies in the statement, also found in chapter 7, that
no dharma can be grasped or expressed in words. In consequence
none of the saints can grasp a fruit as his own. For the true
nature of any object a Saint could obtain is unconditioned
emptiness, and the assumption of a separate subject, or 'self',
as the partaker or owner of the fruit, would also be clearly
erroneous.

**9a. The Lord asked: What do you think, Subhuti, does it
occur to the Streamwinner, 'by me has the fruit of a
Streamwinner been attained'? Subhuti replied: No indeed,
O Lord. And why? Because, O Lord, he has not won any
dharma. Therefore is he called a Stream-winner. No
sight-object has been won, no sounds, smells, tastes,
touchables, or objects of mind. That is why he is called a
'Streamwinner'. If, O Lord, it would occur to a Streamwinner, 'by me has a Streamwinner's fruit been attained',
then that would be in him a seizing on a self, seizing on a
being, seizing on a soul, seizing on a person—9b. The
Lord asked: What do you think, Subhuti, does it then
occur to the Once-Returner, 'by me has the fruit of a
Once-Returner been attained'?—Subhuti replied: No
indeed, O Lord. And why? Because there is not any
dharma that has won Once-Returnership. That is why he
is called a 'Once-Returner'.—9c. The Lord asked: What
do you think, Subhuti, does it then occur to the Never-
Returner 'by me has the fruit of a Never-Returner been
attained'?—Subhuti replied: No indeed, O Lord. And why?**

Because there is not any dharma that has won Never Returnership. Therefore is he called a 'Never-Returner'. —9d. The Lord asked: What do you think, Subhuti, does it then occur to the Arhat, 'by me has Arhatship been attained'?—Subhuti: No indeed, O Lord. And why? Because no dharma is called 'Arhat'. That is why he is called an Arhat. If, O Lord, it would occur to an Arhat, 'by me has Arhatship been attained', then that would be in him a seizing on a self, seizing on a being, seizing on a soul, seizing on a person.—9e. And why? I am, O Lord, the one whom the Tathagata, the Arhat, the Fully Enlightened One has pointed out as the foremost of those who dwell in Peace. I am, O Lord, an Arhat free from greed. And yet, O Lord, it does not occur to me, 'an Arhat am I and free from greed'. If, O Lord, it could occur to me that I have attained Arhatship, then the Tathagata would not have declared of me that 'Subhuti, this son of good family, who is the foremost of those who dwell in Peace, does not dwell anywhere; that is why he is called "a dweller in Peace, a dweller in Peace"'.

The division of the supramundane path into four stages, each marked by a distinctive type of Saint, is a venerable ingredient of the whole Buddhist tradition. At present we look at these dwellers in the transcendental realms from such a distance, that they all may seem pretty much the same to us. It will nevertheless help us to understand the meaning of the text if we attend to the standard definitions of the four types of Saints: A 'Streamwinner' is one who forsakes three fetters, i.e. the view of individuality, the contagion by mere rule and ritual, and doubt, or perplexity. A 'Once-Returner' is one who 'attenuates' sensuous greed and ill-will, while a 'Never-Returner' manages to get quite rid of them. An 'Arhat' finally forsakes the five 'higher' fetters, i.e. greed for the world of form, greed for the formless world, excitedness, conceit and ignorance.

In 9a–d this lore is confronted with the dharmic facts, and found wanting. The word **dharma** here means 'a really existing thing'. 9e then refers to a famous passage in the Scriptures of all Hinayana schools, where the Buddha enumerates his eighty chief disciples as being, each one, **the foremost** in some distinctive spiritual achievement. Sariputra there is the one foremost in 'wisdom', meaning Abhidharma analysis (see p. 81). In the Sutras on the 'Perfection of Wisdom', it is, however, Subhuti, a secondary figure in Theravadin and Sarvastivadin writings, who is held to be most qualified to expound 'perfect wisdom' and 'emptiness' (*A* xvi 306, xxvii 454). *Anguttara Nikaya* (1 24) names him as the disciple who won Arhatship on the basis of meditation on friendliness and who, teaching the dharma without distinction and limitations, is the 'chief of those who live remote and in peace'.

What then is this **dwelling in Peace** in which Subhuti is said to excel? The Sanskrit *a-raṇā*, is one of those words with manifold meanings in which these Sutras abound. The word may denote freedom from strife, battle, or fighting, i.e. harmlessness; or freedom from passion and any kind of defilement, i.e. purity; or it may also mean that Subhuti lived in solitude, retired from the world, in a remote forest, in quietude and peace. A man is 'peaceful' if he has inward peace of mind and if he behaves peacefully towards others. Subhuti's deep insight is the fine flower of his friendly behaviour.

'I am an Arhat free from greed.' It was customary for Arhats to testify to the fact that they had achieved Arhatship. So we read in *Divyavadana* (p. 424) that, 'when the Ven. Vitasoka had attained Arhatship, he experienced the happiness and joy of emancipation, and he thought to himself, "I am indeed an Arhat"'. Likewise, Ashvaghosha in his beautiful poem on *Saundarananda* describes how Nanda the Fair 'related to the Buddha his success in attaining his object', and said (xviii 10): 'My births are now extinct. I live, as one should do, from practice of true Dharma. My tasks are all accomplished. What had to be done I have done. Still in the world I am, no longer can the world affect me!'

3b. *The Bodhisattva's thought of Enlightenment*

The career of a Bodhisattva begins, as we saw at chapter 3, with the 'thought of enlightenment', which is the vow to win full enlightenment for the benefit of all beings. In the life of Shakyamuni, 'the historical Buddha', this happened when he met the Buddha Dipankara, his twenty-fourth predecessor, from whom he received the assurance that he was destined for Buddhahood.

10a. The Lord asked: What do you think, Subhuti, is there any dharma which the Tathagata has learned from Dipankara, the Tathagata, the Arhat, the fully Enlightened One? Subhuti replied: Not so, O Lord, there is not.

The **Tathagata** who **learned dharma from Dipankara** is the Buddha Shakyamuni, who speaks here.[1] One might infer that Shakyamuni at that time 'learned', 'accepted', 'received' or 'took over' some dharma from Dipankara, because, if he had not done so, how could he have formed the desire to emulate Dipankara, by becoming a fully enlightened Buddha, who is one who has understood the Dharma? This inference would, how-ever, contradict the teaching of chapter 9, according to which there is no such thing as a dharma, and in actual fact Shakya-muni received no dharma from Dipankara—he heard no doctrine, and no real entity passed over into him.

3c. *The Bodhisattva and his Pure Land*

The Sutra next considers the eighth stage of a Bodhisattva's career. On the seventh he has fully understood perfect wisdom. This sets free his 'skill in means', which in its turn gives him sovereignty over the world. As the sovereign 'king of Dharma' he can now perfect the beings in a chosen part of the universe, which he slowly transforms into a Pure Land.

10b. The Lord said: If any Bodhisattva would say, 'I will create harmonious Buddhafields', he would speak falsely. And why? 'The harmonies of Buddhafields, the harmonies of Buddhafields', Subhuti, as no-harmonies have they been taught by the Tathagata. Therefore he spoke of 'harmonious Buddhafields'.

A **Buddhafield** is a part of the world in which a Buddha matures beings. As a **harmonious** structure it is compared to an orderly and well-arranged military array. In contradistinc-

---

[1] For the story of the meeting between Shakyamuni and Dipankara see *Mahāvastu*, I 231–9 and my *Buddhist Scriptures*, Penguin Classics.

tion to an ordinary, defiled world such as ours, in a 'Pure Land' all is beauty and order (see *B* 154-5). 'Field' has the same connotation as in 'Elysian Fields'. The term **create** should not be pressed too closely. The Sanskrit *niṣpādayati* also means to 'accomplish, perfect, achieve, ripen and mature'. The force of their meritorious karma enables the Bodhisattvas to realize, or to bring to perfection, a Pure Land, an unworldly world, a 'heaven' or 'paradise' which offers ideal conditions for rapid spiritual progress. It is here assumed that also the material world is a reflex of karma, and that the spiritual maturity of beings determines their living conditions.

For two reasons the Bodhisattva would **speak falsely**, i.e. against the facts, if he were to say, **'I will perfect harmonious Buddhafields'**: (1) Any statement which contains the word 'I' is *ipso facto* false, because in the real world nothing corresponds to it. (2) A Buddhafield is no material or perceptible fact, and its harmony is not an objective arrangement. It has a quasi-sensory appearance as the by-product of a Buddha's meditative gnosis, but in reality it is no more than a mental construction.

3d. The Bodhisattva's Final Nirvana

We now come to the last stage a Bodhisattva can reach, his final Nirvana. This is technically known as *apratiṣṭhita-nirvāṇa*, the Nirvana which is 'without support', or which is 'not permanently fixed'. It is often defined in Mahayana texts. Two quotations will suffice. The *Perfection of Wisdom in 8,000 Lines* (ii 37) says: 'Nowhere has the Tathagata taken his stand; for his mind has not anywhere sought for a support. He has stood neither in the conditioned, nor in the unconditioned, nor has he emerged from them.' The *Mahayana-samgraha* (p. 259) is more explicit: The aim of Bodhisattvas is the Nirvana which is 'not permanently fixed', which does not exclude the Samsara. For they do not, like ordinary people, opt for Samsara, nor do they, like Disciples and Pratyekabuddhas, wish to escape into Nirvana. They do not leave or abandon the samsaric world, but it no longer has the power to defile them.

10c. Therefore then, Subhuti, the Bodhisattva, the great being, should produce an unsupported thought, i.e. a

thought which is nowhere supported, a thought un-supported by sights, sounds, smells, tastes, touchables or mind-objects.

It is said that Huineng, sixth patriarch of the Southern Zen sect, won enlightenment through meditating on this very passage. So at least we read in the *Platform Sutra* (T 2008), although the Tang version (T 2007) is silent on the point. It is well known that the Zen school uses the word 'enlightenment' in a manner peculiar to itself, which differs from that of all other Buddhists, the 'Diamond Sutra' included. But that much is clear that the ability to raise one's mind to these heights of non-attachment is equivalent to the conquest of emancipation, whether temporary or permanent. For beginners the phrase used in chapter 10c can be further clarified by considering the synonyms and alternative translations of the term **unsupported** (21 are listed on pp. 95–6 of my Rome edition of the *Vajracche-dihā*). Once this rather elementary task is performed, one would next have to describe the meditations by which this state of mind is made into a living reality on successive stages of spiritual development. There is no space here for any of this. In this context it is sufficient to say that the **thought** which the Bodhisattva should **produce**, or raise, is a completely free thought, which depends on no object or motive. It is the white heat of wisdom intent on the luminous transparency of the Void. In Tibetan terms, it is Vajradhara, the Ādibuddha, in union with his consort, the Prajñāpāramitā.

10a considered the Bodhisattva as the recipient of Dharma, 10b as the King of Dharma, and now 10c as the Dharmabody. The cryptic sentences which follow are meant to stress the all-pervading greatness of the Dharmabody.

Suppose, Subhuti, there were a man endowed with a body, a huge body, so that he had a personal existence like Sumeru, king of mountains. Would that, Subhuti, be a huge personal existence? Subhuti replied: Yes, huge, O Lord, huge, O Well-Gone, would his personal existence be. And why so? 'Personal existence, personal existence', as no-existence has that been taught by the Tathagata;

for not, O Lord, is that existence or non-existence. Therefore is it called 'personal existence'.

The clumsy term **personal existence** corresponds to *ātma-bhāva*. At chapter 13*e* and 15*a* I have translated the same compound as 'all their belongings'. According to Buddhaghosa, 'personal existence' 'may mean (1) the body; or, (2) all the five skandhas together. For it is dependent on them that the mere concept (of a self or person) comes about, after the usage of foolish people who are in the habit of saying, "this is myself".' It is that which is regarded as belonging to a self, the existence round a self, the sum total of all that seems to be built round a self. **Sumeru,** mentioned also in chapter 24, is a mountain forming the centre of the world. Submerged by the sea to a depth of 84,000 leagues, it rises above the surface to the same height. The Dharmabody of the Sage is obviously **not existence** and **not non-existence.** But the whole passage loses its point in translation, and we had better pass on.

3e. The merit derived from Perfect Wisdom

The four major sections of the Sutra conclude each with a few remarks on the merit which forms the basis of the spiritual achievements discussed, and which is traced back to the teachings of this Sutra. Chapters 11 and 12 in this way correspond to chapter 8.

11. The Lord asked: What do you think, Subhuti, if there were as many Ganges rivers as there are grains of sand in the large river Ganges, would the grains of sand in them be many?—Subhuti replied: Those Ganges rivers would indeed be many, much more so the grains of sand in them.—The Lord said: This is what I announce to you, Subhuti, this is what I make known to you,—if some woman or man had filled with the seven precious things as many world systems as there are grains of sand in those Ganges rivers, and would give them as a gift to the Tathagatas, Arhats, fully Enlightened Ones—what do you think, Subhuti, would that woman or man on the strength of that beget a great heap of merit?—Subhuti replied: Great, O Lord, great O Well-Gone, would that heap of

merit be, immeasurable and incalculable.—The Lord said: But if a son or daughter of good family had taken from this discourse on dharma but one stanza of four lines, and were to demonstrate and illuminate it to others, then they would on the strength of that beget a still greater heap of merit, immeasurable and incalculable. 12. Moreover, Subhuti, that spot of earth where one has taken from this discourse on dharma but one stanza of four lines, taught or illumined it, that spot of earth will be a veritable shrine for the whole world with its gods, men and Asuras. What then should we say of those who will bear in mind this discourse on dharma in its entirety, who will recite, study, and illuminate it in full detail for others! Most wonderfully blest, Subhuti, they will be! And on that spot of earth, Subhuti, either the Teacher dwells, or a sage representing him.

This is what I announce to you, etc.—a formula often used for formal pronouncements by a Buddha.—The saying about the **shrine,** *caitya*, is repeated in chapter 15c. It is taken over from the Version in 8,000 lines (iii 56–7): 'The place in which one takes up, bears in mind, preaches, studies, spreads, demonstrates, expounds, explains and repeats this Perfection of Wisdom, in it beings cannot be hurt by men or ghosts, nor can they be injured or overpowered by them, except as a punishment for their past deeds. Because this Perfection of Wisdom makes the spot of earth where it is, into a true shrine for beings, worthy of being worshipped and adored—into a shelter for beings who come to it, a refuge, a place of rest, and final relief. This is another advantage which Perfect Wisdom confers even here and now'. According to B. C. Law, *caitya* is the most general name for any sanctuary, and it may refer to a Stupa, a *vihāra*, an assembly hall, a tree, a memorial stone, a holy relic or object, or even an image. A shrine is a sacred place set apart, and it should be honoured with gifts of flowers, and so on. In past ages these shrines were something to reckon with. Respect for them assured the prosperity of nations, and they were inviolate sanctuaries for people in fear for their lives.— **The Teacher** is the Buddha. **A Sage,** *guru*, is a spiritual preceptor.

4. THE FIRST ENDING

The source of this merit is the 'discourse on dharma', which is now named. The Sutra in its first form probably finished at this point.

13a. Subhuti asked: What then, O Lord, is this discourse on dharma, and how should I bear it in mind?—The Lord replied: This discourse on dharma, Subhuti, is called 'Wisdom which has gone beyond', and as such should you bear it in mind!

It is noteworthy that the title of the 'Diamond Sutra' is here simply 'Perfection of Wisdom'. Kumarajiva, it is true, has 'Adamantine Perfection of Wisdom', but not so the Sanskrit.

★　★　★　★

The *second part* of the Sutra presents the commentator with exceptional and so far insuperable difficulties. It is not impossible that one day someone may succeed in offering a satisfactory explanation. None has yet been found. Even Asanga, Vasubandhu and Kamalaśīla were often at a loss to account for the logical sequence behind the argument, and their comments are apt to be unconvincing, laboured and over-ingenious. My own commentary, based on their suggestions, was rewritten a number of times. Even in its final form it failed to ring true, and I must agree with my friends who pronounced it to be unhelpful, inconclusive, tedious, uninspiring and positively confusing. Far from adding to the understanding of the Sutra's spiritual message, this part of the commentary actually obscures it, though it might have some value for philologists concerned with the construction of the Sanskrit sentences.

Our bewilderments are perhaps due to invincible obtuseness. It is equally possible that they derive from the state of the text which has been transmitted to us. Far from representing a coherent whole, the second part of the *Diamond Sutra* may very well be no more than a chance medley of stray sayings. Scholars who are familiar with the conditions of literary composition in Buddhist India, and who have considered the frequent repetitions and violent transitions in this part of the

Sutra, are inclined to believe that reciters at various times added a passage here or there, and that, what is more, the scribes at one time misplaced some of the palm leaves, and also added glosses from the margin into the text. In that case the sequence of the argument would be determined by a series of mechanical accidents, and I have been ·content with a bare translation of chapters 13 to 29, adding a few headlines to serve as tentative indications of the problems discussed, which are nearly always variations on the topics of the first part. Chapters 30 to 32 then again break new ground, and the commentary is therefore resumed when we come to them.

5. TRANSCENDENTALITY

5a. *The dialectical nature of reality.*

And why? Just that which the Tathagata has taught as the wisdom which has gone beyond, just that He has taught as not gone beyond. Therefore is it called 'Wisdom which has gone beyond'. 13b. What do you think, Subhuti, is there any dharma which the Tathagata has taught?— Subhuti replied: No indeed, O Lord, there is not.— 13c. The Lord said: When, Subhuti, you consider the number of particles of dust in this world system of 1,000 million worlds—would they be many?—Subhuti replied: Yes, O Lord. Because what was taught as par- ticles of dust by the Tathagata, as no-particles that was taught by the Tathagata. Therefore are they called 'particles of dust'. And this world-system the Tathagata has taught as no-system. Therefore is it called a 'world system'.—13d. The Lord asked: What do you think, Subhuti, can the Tathagata be seen by means of the thirty- two marks of the superman?—Subhuti replied: No indeed, O Lord. And why? Because those thirty-two marks of the superman which were taught by the Tatha- gata, they are really no-marks. Therefore are they called 'the thirty-two marks of the superman'.

5b. *The supreme excellence of this teaching.*

13e. The Lord said: And again, Subhuti, suppose a woman or a man were to renounce all their belongings as many

times as there are grains of sand in the river Ganges;
and suppose that someone else, after taking from
this discourse on Dharma but one stanza of four lines,
would demonstrate it to others. Then this latter on the
strength of that would beget a greater heap of merit,
immeasurable and incalculable.

14*a*. Thereupon the impact of Dharma moved the Venerable Subhuti to tears. Having wiped away his tears, he
thus spoke to the Lord: It is wonderful, O Lord, it is exceedingly wonderful, O Well-Gone, how well the Tathagata has taught this discourse on Dharma. Through it
cognition has been produced in me. Not have I ever before
heard such a discourse on Dharma. Most wonderfully
blest will be those who, when this Sutra is being taught,
will produce a true perception. And that which is true perception, that is indeed no perception. Therefore the
Tathagata teaches, 'true perception, true perception'.—
14*b*. It is not difficult for me to accept and believe this
discourse on Dharma when it is being taught. But those
beings who will be in a future period, in the last time, in
the last epoch, in the last 500 years, at the time of the
collapse of the good doctrine, and who, O Lord, will take
up this discourse on Dharma, bear it in mind, recite it,
study it, and illuminate it in full detail for others, these
will be most wonderfully blest.—14*c*. In them, however, no
perception of a self will take place, or of a being, a soul,
or a person. And why? That, O Lord, which is perception
of self, that is indeed no perception. That which is perception of a being, a soul or a person, that is indeed no
perception. And why? Because the Buddhas, the Lords
have left all perceptions behind.

14*d*. The Lord said: So it is, Subhuti. Most wonderfully
blest will be those beings who, on hearing this Sutra,
will not tremble, nor be frightened, or terrified. And why?
The Tathagata has taught this as the highest (paramā)
perfection (pāramitā). And what the Tathagata teaches
as the highest perfection, that also the innumerable
(aparimāna) Blessed Buddhas do teach. Therefore is it
called the 'highest perfection'.

5c. Selfless Patience and perfect inner freedom

14e. Moreover, Subhuti, the Tathagata's perfection of patience is really no perfection. And why? Because, Subhuti, when the king of Kalinga cut my flesh from every limb, at that time I had no perception of a self, of a being, of a soul, or a person. And why? If, Subhuti, at that time I had had a perception of self, I would also have had a perception of ill-will at that time. And so, if I had had a perception of a being, of a soul, or of a person. With my superknowledge I recall that in the past I have for five hundred births led the life of a sage devoted to patience. Then also have I had no perception of a self, a being, a soul, or a person.

Therefore then, Subhuti, the Bodhi-being, the great being, after he has got rid of all perceptions, should raise his thought to the utmost, right and perfect enlightenment. He should produce a thought which is unsupported by forms, sounds, smells, tastes, touchables, or mind-objects, unsupported by dharma, unsupported by no-dharma, unsupported by anything. And why? All supports have actually no support. It is for this reason that the Tathagata teaches: By an unsupported Bodhisattva should a gift be given, not by one who is supported by forms, sounds, smells, tastes, touchables, or mind-objects.

5d. The existence and non-existence of beings

14f. And further, Subhuti, it is for the weal of all beings that a Bodhisattva should give gifts in this manner. And why? This perception of a being, Subhuti, that is just a non-perception. Those all-beings of whom the Tathagata has spoken, they are indeed no-beings. And why? Because the Tathagata speaks in accordance with reality, speaks the truth, speaks of what is, not otherwise. A Tathagata does not speak falsely.

5e. Truth and Falsehood

14g. But nevertheless, Subhuti, with regard to that dharma which the Tathagata has fully known and demonstrated, on account of that there is neither truth nor fraud.

In darkness a man could not see anything. Just so should be viewed a Bodhisattva who has fallen among things, and who, fallen among things, renounces a gift. A man with eyes would, when the night becomes light and the sun has arisen, see manifold forms. Just so should be viewed a Bodhisattva who has not fallen among things, and who, without having fallen among things, renounces a gift.

5f. The Merit acquired, its presuppositions and results

14h. Furthermore, Subhuti, those sons and daughters of good family who will take up this discourse on Dharma, will bear it in mind, recite, study, and illuminate it in full detail for others, they have been known, Subhuti, by the Tathagata with his Buddha-cognition, they have been seen, Subhuti, by the Tathagata with his Buddha-eye, they have been fully known by the Tathagata. All these beings, Subhuti, will beget and acquire an immeasurable and incalculable heap of merit.—**15a.** And if, Subhuti, a woman or man should renounce in the morning all their belongings as many times as there are grains of sand in the river Ganges, and if they should do likewise at noon and in the evening, and if in this way they should renounce all their belongings for many hundreds of thousands of millions of milliards of aeons; and someone else, on hearing this discourse on Dharma, would not reject it; then the latter would on the strength of that beget a greater heap of merit, immeasurable and incalculable. What then should we say of him who, after writing it, would learn it, bear it in mind, recite, study and illuminate it in full detail for others?

15b. Moreover, Subhuti, (1) unthinkable and (2) incomparable is this discourse on Dharma. (3) The Tathagata has taught it for the weal of beings who have set out in the best, in the most excellent vehicle. Those who will take up this discourse on Dharma, bear it in mind, recite, study and illuminate it in full detail for others, the

Tathagata has known them with his Buddha-cognition, the Tathagata has seen them with his Buddha-eye, the Tathagata has fully known them. All these beings, Subhuti, will be blest with an immeasurable heap of merit, they will be blest with a heap of merit unthinkable, incomparable, measureless and illimitable. All these beings, Subhuti, will carry along an equal share of enlightenment. And why? (4) Because it is not possible, Subhuti, that this discourse on Dharma could be heard by beings of inferior resolve, nor by such as have a self in view, a being, a soul, or a person. Nor can beings who have not taken the pledge of Bodhi-beings either hear this discourse on Dharma, or take it up, bear it in mind, recite or study it. That cannot be.

15c. (1) Moreover, Subhuti, the spot of earth where this Sutra will be revealed, that spot of earth will be worthy of worship by the whole world with its Gods, men and Asuras, worthy of being saluted respectfully, worthy of being honoured by circumambulation,— like a shrine will be that spot of earth.—16a. And yet Subhuti, those sons and daughters of good family, who will take up these very Sutras, and will bear them in mind, recite and study them, they will be humbled,— well humbled they will be! And why? The impure deeds which these beings have done in their former lives, and which are liable to lead them into the states of woe,— in this very life they will, by means of that humiliation, (2) annul those impure deeds of their former lives, and (3) they will reach the enlightenment of a Buddha.— 16b. With my superknowledge, Subhuti, I recall that in the past period, long before Dipankara, the Tathagata, Arhat, fully Enlightened One, during incalculable, quite incalculable aeons, I gave satisfaction by loyal service to 84,000 million milliards of Buddhas, without ever becoming again estranged from them. But the heap of merit, Subhuti, from the satisfaction I gave to those Buddhas and Lords without again becoming estranged from them—compared with the heap of merit of those who in the last time, the last epoch, the last five hundred years, at the time of the collapse of the good doctrine, will take up these very Sutras, bear them in mind, recite and study them, and will illuminate them in full detail for others, it does not approach one hundredth part, not one thousandth part, nor a one hundred thousandth part, not a ten millionth part, nor a one hundred millionth part, nor a 100,000 millionth part. It does not bear number, nor fraction, nor counting, nor similarity, nor comparison, nor resemblance.—16c. (4) If moreover, Subhuti, I were to teach the heap of merit of those sons and daughters of good family, and how great a heap of merit they will at that time beget and acquire, beings would become frantic and confused. Since, however, Subhuti, the Tathagata has taught this discourse on Dharma as unthinkable, so just an unthinkable karma-result should be expected from it.

6. THE BODHISATTVAS

In chapter 17 the Sutra now veers back to its beginning. The question of chapter 2 is repeated, and so is the answer of chapter 3. 17a–d successively considers three stages of the Bodhisattva's career, just as chapters 3 to 5, and again chapter 10 did. With the absence of a real entity for its leading idea, chapter 17 once more goes over the old ground. 17a corresponds to 3; 17b to 10a; 17d to 7, 14g and the end of 8; 17e to 10c, and 17g to 10b. I have marked the literal repetitions by placing them into double brackets.

6a. The Bodhisattva's Vow

17a. [(Subhuti asked: How, O Lord, should one set out in the Bodhisattva-vehicle stand, how progress, how control his thoughts?—The Lord replied: Here, Subhuti, someone who has set out in the Bodhisattva-vehicle should produce a thought in this manner: 'all beings I must lead to Nirvana, into that Realm of Nirvana which leaves nothing behind; and yet, after beings have thus been led to Nirvana, no being at all has been led to Nirvana'. And why? If in a Bodhisattva the notion of a 'being' should

take place, he could not be called a 'Bodhi-being'. And
likewise if the notion of a soul, or a person should take
place in him.)] And why? He who has set out in the
Bodhisattva-vehicle—he is not one of the dharmas.

6b. *The Bodhisattva's state of mind when he met Dipankara.*

17b. What do you think Subhuti, is there any dharma by
which the Tathagata, when he was with Dipankara the
Tathagata, has fully known the utmost, right and perfect
enlightenment?—Subhuti replied: There is not any
dharma by which the Tathagata, when he was with the
Tathagata Dipankara, has fully known the utmost, right
and perfect enlightenment.—The Lord said: It is for this
reason that the Tathagata Dipankara then predicted of
me: 'You, young Brahmin, will be in a future period a
Tathagata, Arhat, fully Enlightened, by the name of
Shakyamuni!'

6c. *The Bodhisattva at the end of his career*

17c. And why? 'Tathagata', Subhuti, is synonymous with
true Suchness (tathatā).—**17d.** And whosoever, Subhuti,
were to say, 'The Tathagata has fully known the utmost,
right and perfect enlightenment', he would speak falsely.
And why? [(There is not any dharma by which the
Tathagata has fully known the utmost, right and perfect
enlightenment. And that dharma which the Tathagata
has fully known and demonstrated, on account of that
there is neither truth nor fraud.)] Therefore the Tathagata
teaches, 'all dharmas are the Buddha's own and special
dharmas'. And why? 'All-dharmas', Subhuti, have as
no-dharmas been taught by the Tathagata. Therefore all
dharmas are called the Buddha's own and special
dharmas.—**17e.** ([Just as a man, Subhuti, might be
endowed with a body, a huge body.)]—Subhuti said:
That man of whom the Tathagata spoke as 'endowed
with a body, a huge body', as a no-body he has been
taught by the Tathagata. Therefore is he called, 'endowed with a body, a huge body'.

6d. The Bodhisattva's attitude to his tasks

17f. The Lord said: So it is, Subhuti. The Bodhisattva who would say, 'I will lead beings to Nirvana', he should not be called a 'Bodhi-being'. And why? Is there, Subhuti, any dharma named 'Bodhi-being'?—Subhuti replied: No indeed, O Lord.—The Lord said: Because of that the Tathagata teaches, 'selfless are all dharmas, they have not the character of living beings, they are without a living soul, without personality'.—17g. [(If any Bodhi-sattva should say, 'I will create harmonious Buddha-fields')], he likewise should not be called a Bodhi-being. [(And why? 'The harmonies of Buddhafields, the harmonies of Buddhafields', Subhuti, as no-harmonies have they been taught by the Tathagata. Therefore he spoke of 'harmonious Buddhafields'.)]—17h. The Bodhi-sattva, however, Subhuti, who is intent on 'without self are the dharmas, without self are the dharmas', him the Tathagata, the Arhat, the fully Enlightened One has declared to be a Bodhi-being, a great being.

7. THE BUDDHAS

7a. The Buddha's Five Eyes

18a. What do you think, Subhuti, does the fleshly eye of the Tathagata exist?—Subhuti replied: So it is, O Lord, the fleshly eye of the Tathagata does exist.—The Lord asked: What do you think, Subhuti, does the Tathagata's heavenly eye exist, his wisdom eye, his Dharma-eye, his Buddha-eye?—Subhuti replied: So it is, O Lord, the heavenly eye of the Tathagata does exist, and so does his wisdom eye, his Dharma-eye and his Buddha-eye.

7b. The Buddha's superknowledge of others' thoughts.

18b. The Lord said: What do you think, Subhuti, has the Tathagata used the phrase, 'as many grains of sand as there are in the great river Ganges'?—Subhuti replied: So it is, O Lord, so it is, O Well-Gone! The Tathagata has done so.—The Lord asked: What do you think, Subhuti, if there were as many Ganges rivers as there are grains

of sand in the great river Ganges, and if there were as
many world systems as there are grains of sand in them,
would those world systems be many?—Subhuti replied:
So it is, O Lord, so it is, O Well-Gone, these world systems
would be many.—The Lord said: As many beings as
there are in these world systems, of them I know, in my
wisdom, the manifold trends of thought. And why?
'Trends of thought, trends of thought', Subhuti, as no-
trends have they been taught by the Tathagata. Therefore
are they called 'trends of thought'. And why? Past thought
is not got at; future thought is not got at; present thought
is not got at.

7c. The Buddha's Merit is no Merit

19. What do you think, Subhuti, if a son or daughter of
good family had filled this world system of 1,000 million
worlds with the seven precious things, and then gave it as
a gift to the Tathagatas, the Arhats, the fully Enlightened
Ones, would they on the strength of that beget a great
heap of merit?—Subhuti replied: they would, O Lord,
they would, O Well-Gone!—The Lord said: So it is,
Subhuti, so it is. On the strength of that this son or
daughter of good family would beget a great heap of
merit, immeasurable and incalculable. But if, on the
other hand, there were such a thing as a heap of merit, the
Tathagata would not have spoken of a 'heap of merit'.

7d. The Buddha's Physical Body

20a. What do you think, Subhuti, is the Tathagata to be
seen by means of the accomplishment of his form-body?
Subhuti replied: No indeed, O Lord, the Tathagata is not
to be seen by means of the accomplishment of his form-
body. And why? 'Accomplishment of his form-body,
accomplishment of his form-body', this, O Lord, has been
taught by the Tathagata as no-accomplishment. Therefore is it called 'accomplishment of his form-body'.—
20b. The Lord asked: What do you think, Subhuti, is the
Tathagata to be seen through his possession of marks?—
Subhuti replied: No indeed, O Lord. And why? This
possession of marks, O Lord, which has been taught by

the Tathagata, as a no-possession of no-marks this has
been taught by the Tathagata. Therefore is it called
'possession of marks'.

7e. *The Buddha's teaching*

21a. The Lord asked: What do you think, Subhuti, does it
occur to the Tathagata, 'by me has Dharma been demonstrated'? Whosoever, Subhuti, would say, 'the Tathagata
has demonstrated Dharma', he would speak falsely, he
would misrepresent me by seizing on what is not there.
And why? 'Demonstration of dharma, demonstration of
dharma', Subhuti, there is not any dharma which could
be got at as a demonstration of dharma.

21b. Subhuti asked: Are there, O Lord, any beings in the
future, in the last time, in the last epoch, in the last
500 years, at the time of the collapse of the good doctrine
who, on hearing such dharmas, will truly believe?—The
Lord replied: They, Subhuti, are neither beings nor
no-beings. And why? 'Beings, beings', Subhuti, the
Tathagata has taught that they are all no-beings. Therefore has he spoken of 'all beings'.

7f. *The Buddha's Dharma*

22. What do you think, Subhuti, is there any dharma by
which the Tathagata has fully known the utmost, right
and perfect enlightenment?—Subhuti replied: No indeed,
O Lord, there is not any dharma by which the Tathagata
has fully known the utmost, right and perfect enlightenment.—The Lord said: So it is, Subhuti, so it is. Not even
the least (anu) dharma is there found or got at. Therefore
is it called 'utmost (anuttara), right and perfect enlightenment'.—23. Furthermore, Subhuti, self-identical (sama)
is that dharma, and nothing is therein at variance
(vishama). Therefore is it called 'utmost, right (samyak)
and perfect (sam-) enlightenment'. Self-identical through
the absence of a self, a being, a soul, or a person, the
utmost, right and perfect enlightenment is fully known
as the totality of all the wholesome dharmas. 'Wholesome
dharmas, wholesome dharmas', Subhuti—yet as no-

dharmas have they been taught by the Tathagata. Therefore are they called 'wholesome dharmas'.

7g. *Once more about the Buddha's Merit*

24. And again, Subhuti, if a woman or man had piled up the seven precious things until their bulk equalled that of all the Sumerus, kings of mountains, in the world system of 1,000 million worlds, and would give them as a gift; and if, on the other hand, a son or daughter of good family would take up from this Prajñāpāramitā, this discourse on Dharma, but one stanza of four lines, and demonstrate it to others, compared with his heap of merit the former heap of merit does not approach one hundredth part, etc., until we come to, it will not bear any comparison.

7h. *The Buddha as a Saviour, and the nature of emancipation.*

25. What do you think, Subhuti, does it occur to a Tathagata, 'by me have beings been set free'? Not thus should you see it, Subhuti! And why? There is not any being whom the Tathagata has set free. Again, if there had been any being whom the Tathagata had set free, then surely there would have been on the part of the Tathagata a seizing of a self, of a being, of a soul, of a person. 'Seizing of a self', as a no-seizing, Subhuti, has that been taught by the Tathagata. And yet the foolish common people have seized upon it. 'Foolish common people', Subhuti, as really no people have they been taught by the Tathagata. Therefore are they called 'foolish common people'.

7i. *The true nature of a Buddha*

26a. What do you think, Subhuti, is the Tathagata to be seen by means of his possession of marks?—Subhuti replied: No indeed, O Lord.—The Lord said: If, Subhuti, the Tathagata could be recognized by his possession of marks, then also the universal monarch would be a Tathagata. Therefore the Tathagata is not to be seen by means of his possession of marks.—Subhuti then said:

As I, O Lord, understand the Lord's teaching, the Tathagata is not to be seen through his possession of
marks.

Further the Lord taught on that occasion the following
stanzas:

> Those who by my form did see me,
> And those who followed me by voice
> Wrong the efforts they engaged in,
> Me those people will not see.

26b. From the Dharma should one see the Buddhas,
From the Dharmabodies comes their guidance.
Yet Dharma's true nature cannot be discerned,
And no one can be conscious of it as an object.

7k. The effectiveness of meritorious deeds

27. What do you think, Subhuti, has the Tathagata fully
known the utmost, right and perfect enlightenment
through his possession of marks? Not so should you see
it, Subhuti. And why? Because the Tathagata could surely
not have fully known the utmost, right and perfect
enlightenment through his possession of marks.

Nor should anyone, Subhuti, say to you, 'those who
have set out in the Bodhisattva-vehicle have conceived
the destruction of a dharma, or its annihilation'. Not so
should you see it, Subhuti! For those who have set out in
the Bodhisattva-vehicle have not conceived the destruction of a dharma, or its annihilation.

28. And again, Subhuti, if a son or daughter of good
family had filled with the seven precious things as many
world systems as there are grains of sand in the river
Ganges, and gave them as a gift to the Tathagatas,
Arhats, fully Enlightened Ones,—and if on the other
hand a Bodhisattva would gain the patient acquiescence
in dharmas which are nothing of themselves and which
fail to be produced, then this latter would on the strength
of that beget a greater heap of merit, immeasurable and
incalculable.

Moreover, Subhuti, the Bodhisattva should not acquire

a heap of merit.—Subhuti said: Surely, O Lord, the Bodhisattva should acquire a heap of merit?—The Lord said: 'Should acquire', Subhuti, not 'should seize upon.' Therefore is it said, 'should acquire'.

29. Whosoever says that the Tathagata goes or comes, stands, sits or lies down, he does not understand the meaning of my teaching. And why? 'Tathagata' is called one who has not gone anywhere, nor come from anywhere. Therefore is he called 'the Tathagata, the Arhat, the fully Enlightened One'.

8. ADVICE TO THE IMPERFECT

8a. *The material world*

30a. And again, Subhuti, if a son or daughter of good family were to grind as many world systems as there are particles of dust in this great world system of 1,000 million worlds, as finely as they can be ground with incalculable vigour, and in fact reduce them to something like a collection of atomic quantities, what do you think, Subhuti, would that be an enormous collection of atomic quantities?—Subhuti replied: So it is, O Lord, so it is, O Well-Gone, enormous would that collection of atomic quantities be! And why? If, O Lord, there had been an enormous collection of atomic quantities, the Lord would not have called it an 'enormous collection of atomic quantities'. And why? What was taught by the Tathagata as a 'collection of atomic quantities', as a no-collection that was taught by the Tathagata. Therefore is it called a 'collection of atomic quantities'.

30b. And what the Tathagata taught as 'the world system of 1,000 million worlds', that he has taught as a no-system. Therefore is it called 'the world system of 1,000 million worlds'. And why? If, O Lord, there had been a world system, that would have been a case of seizing on a material object, and what was taught as 'seizing on a material object' by the Tathagata, just as a no-seizing was that taught by the Tathagata. Therefore is it called 'seizing on a material object'.—The Lord added: And also,

Subhuti, that 'seizing on a material object' is a matter of linguistic convention, a verbal expression without factual content. It is not a dharma nor a no-dharma. And yet the foolish common people have seized upon it.

The principle of the simultaneity of contradictions is now extended to the material world. Overawed by the immensity of the universe outside us, we may well despair of reducing it to emptiness. And our spirit is often weighed down by the mere thought of the mass of matter which seems to escape the spiritual laws in which it feels at home. Spiritual aspirations threaten to be swallowed up by this senseless bulk into a sort of nightmare of meaninglessness. The enormous quantity of matter that we perceive around us, compared with the trembling little flicker of spiritual insight that we perceive within us, seems to tell strongly in favour of a materialistic outlook on life.

But if we look more closely, then we discover that there is no bulk of matter at all, but only thoughts and words. The material world also obeys the laws governing thoughts and statements. These dialectical laws are valid everywhere, even light-years away, and they apply to all that is contained in the immensity of space. These material things have their roots in our own minds, and it is there that they can be uprooted. If you grab at the idea of world-systems and make yourself miserable, allowing them to crush your spirit, it is still a matter of what *you* do, it is still a state of *mind* which worries *you*.

Archimedes once divided the universe up into particles the size of grains of sand, and decided that there would be 10^{63} of them. About twenty years ago I read that the universe contains 10^{79} pairs of ultimate particles, i.e. protons and electrons at that time. I do not know what the present estimate is—and the Sutra is content to describe the number as **enormous**. The things which are composed of atomic dust are not, however, real genuine units, and therefore each one of them is **a non-collection**. And a universe is no more than a fortuitous conglomeration of various elements (see p. 40), and therefore it is really **a no-system**.

Seizing on a material object, the Sanskrit *piṇḍagrāha,* is deliberately ambiguous. The range of the meanings of the word *piṇḍa* is rather wide. It may mean (1) 'lump, ball'; (2) 'morsel of food given in alms'; (3) 'livelihood'; (4) 'body, person, individual'; (5) 'material object'.

A verbal expression without factual content—this is a rather free translation of *avācya*, which at chapter 7 was translated as 'cannot be talked about'. Haribhadra explains that one 'cannot distinguish the various objects to which the different words refer'.—**And yet the foolish common people have seized upon it:** Asanga explains: How is it that the profane believe to grasp that which in reality cannot be grasped? Because they are foolish, the knowledge they possess is merely **a matter of linguistic convention.** Entirely imprisoned in their verbal habits they do not know that all these things, like the notion of mass, etc., are mere conventional expressions, and so they grasp all this in a different way from what it really is, otherwise than it really is.

8b. *Views and Attitudes*

It is therefore not the suppression of either atoms or worlds which leads to enlightenment, but the elimination of the wrong views about them. This theme is now further clarified in chapter 31. Two kinds of false views are mentioned in succession, first the assumption of a self (31*a*), and secondly that of a dharma (31*b*).

31a. And why? Because whosoever would say that the view of a self has been taught by the Tathagata, the view of a being, the view of a living soul, the view of a person, would he, Subhuti, be speaking right?—Subhuti replied: No indeed, O Lord, no indeed, O Well-Gone, he would not be speaking right. And why? That which has been taught by the Tathagata as 'view of self', as a no-view has that been taught by the Tathagata? Therefore is it called 'view of self'.—31b. The Lord said: It is thus, Subhuti, that someone who has set out in the Bodhisattva-vehicle should know all dharmas, view them, be intent on them. And he should know, view and be intent on them in such a way that he does not set up the perception of a dharma. And why? 'Perception of dharma, perception of dharma,'

Subhuti, as no-perception has this been taught by the Tathagata. Therefore is it called 'perception of dharma'.

The **view of self** is in fact a **no-view**, because without a really existing object. **The perception of a dharma** is a **no-perception**, because there is nothing to perceive. Both views have originated from wrong imagination. It is therefore, as Asanga says, 'impossible to win enlightenment by the suppression of either self or dharma, because they do not exist', and can therefore not be suppressed. 'In consequence, both the affirmation of self and dharmas, as well as their negation, derive from the assumption of something unreal and refer to something which is wrongly conceived. Both therefore represent a subtle 'cover' (see p. 95), which must be eliminated by the 'cognition' taught in this Sutra.

8c. The key to supreme knowledge

32a. And finally, Subhuti, if a Bodhisattva, a great being had filled world-systems immeasurable and incalculable with the seven precious things, and gave them as a gift to the Tathagatas, the Arhats, the fully Enlightened Ones,— and if, on the other hand, a son or daughter of good family had taken from this Prajñāpāramitā, this discourse on Dharma, but one stanza of four lines, and were to bear it in mind, demonstrate, recite and study it, and illuminate it in full detail for others, on the strength of that this latter would beget a greater heap of merit, immeasurable and incalculable. And how would he illuminate it? So as not to reveal. Therefore is it said, 'he would illuminate'.

So as not to reveal: The *Prajñāpāramitā* concerns the unconditioned Absolute and Emptiness. This should not be revealed directly, if only for the reason that that cannot be done. It is **illuminated,** or explained, indirectly by stating the wise attitude to conditioned things, as in the **stanza of four lines** which follows. From this Conditioned the Unconditioned is then different, although identical with it (see p. 83). Nevertheless, the verse contains the essential teaching, because, when a complete understanding of conditioned things, and a mastery over them, have been attained, their impurities can no longer defile, and thereby *ipso facto* a state of Nirvana is attained.

When we have realized what conditioned things really are, we will take no more delight in them, will become increasingly purified, become more and more independent of them, and finally cease to rely on them. And that is Nirvana and Emptiness. Kumarajiva's translation makes this connection clear by adding, just before the verse, this sentence: 'When he does not seize upon signs, Suchness remains unmoved.'

> As stars, a fault of vision, as a lamp,
> A mock show, dew drops, or a bubble,
> A dream, a lightning flash, or cloud,
> So should one view what is conditioned.

The characteristics of all conditioned things, or of all the elements of Samsara, should be considered from nine points of view:

1. Like **stars**.

(*a*) Stars are distant and unreachable. One cannot get to them, they are unattainable, as all dharmas are. One cannot lay hands on them, cannot possess them.

(*b*) They are small in size, insignificant, when seen on the background of the vast vacuity of space.

(*c*) They can be seen only when there is no sun. As the stars are no longer visible when the sun comes to shine, so also the things of the world are seen only in the darkness of ignorance, and are no longer noticed when the normal mental reactions to them come to a stop, after the true non-dual cognition of the Absolute has taken place. All mental elements, as Vasubandhu says, disappear when right cognition is realized, just as the stars disappear when the sun shines. They become invisible, and all views cease.

(*d*) Alternatively, the word *tārakā* can also mean 'meteor'. In that case, because of its short life, the meaning is analogous to that of no. 8, the 'lightning flash'.

2. The second item, **a fault of vision**, *timira*, may mean 'darkness, blindness, a cataract'. The ignorant are often compared to people blinded by darkness (see chapter 14*g*). 'Ignorance overpowers beings through lack of vision, or through false vision, just as a cataract overpowers the eyes' (*VM* 583). 'Ignorance' means that (*a*) intellectually, one sees nothing,

for ignorance is a condition unfavourable to knowledge; (b) emotionally, one feels lost and terrified; (c) volitionally, one knocks against things, stumbles about, is irritated, and wants to get to the light. The world as it appears to the ignorant is like a hallucination which springs from an eye-disease, and the things which are wrongly perceived are about as real as the spots which liverish people see in front of their eyes, or as the hairs which a monk afflicted with *timira* believes to see in his almsbowl.

3. The simile of the **lamp** illustrates two aspects of this world of ours: (a) A lamp goes on burning only as long as fuel is fed into it. So also this world continues only while we have cravings. When craving ceases to supply the drive, the world will come to an end. (b) In their Indian form, before glass chimneys came to be used, lamps were liable to be blown out by the wind. Likewise one conditioned thing is very easily disturbed by others, and the continued existence of conditioned dharmas is all the time distinctly precarious.

4. Furthermore, the appearance of this world is like a **mock show**, a magical illusion. Like a magical show it deceives, deludes and defrauds us, is false when compared with ultimate reality. Things, as Vasubandhu says, are not a trustworthy support. It is assumed that the world of conditioned things is manufactured by ignorance, and Nagarjuna, in his great commentary, shows that ignorance and the products of the magician's art have the following attributes in common: They are neither inside a person, nor outside, nor both inside or outside; they can therefore not be localized with reference to persons; there is nothing real that has been either produced or destroyed; no real event, with an essence of its own, has taken place. And yet, although ignorance is not real, it is the condition for all kinds of activity. Similarly, the musical instruments conjured up by magic are empty, deceptive, without reality, without objective basis, and yet one can hear their music and can see them.

5. The **dew-drops** may also be 'hoar-frost'. That depends on the climate. Each thing is as evanescent as the dew-drops which soon evaporate under the sun's rays.

6. Like a **bubble** each experience bursts soon, and it can be enjoyed only for a moment. In Buddhist tradition, the bubble, a particularly unsubstantial entity, is usually related to the skandha of feeling. Dependent on three factors—enjoyer, enjoyable thing, and enjoyment—all joys quickly burst apart. And the same holds good of painful feelings also.

7. Only the enlightened are awake to reality as it is; compared with their vision of true reality, our normal experience is that of a **dream,** unreal and not to be taken seriously. Nagarjuna, in his great commentary (*Mpps* pp. 373–5) gives the following explanation of the simile of the dream: '(*a*) There is no reality in a dream, and yet, while one dreams, one believes in the reality of the things one sees in the dream. After one has woken up one recognizes the falseness of the dream and laughs at oneself. Just so a man who is plunged into the dreamy state which results from his fettered existence, has a belief in things which do not exist. But when he has found the Path, then, at the moment of enlightenment, he understands that there is no reality in them and he laughs at himself. (*b*) A dreamer, by the force of his dream, sees a thing where there is nothing. Just so a man, by the force of the dreamy state which results from ignorance, believes in the existence of all sorts of things which do not exist, such as I and mine, male and female, etc. (*c*) In a dream one rejoices although there is nothing enjoyable, one is angry although there is nothing to annoy, one is frightened although there is nothing to frighten. So do the beings with regard to the things of the world.' Therefore, like the things seen in a dream, the dharmas, although they do not exist, are nevertheless seen and heard and one is aware of them.

8. Like **a lightning flash** each event is short-lived. Lasting but one brief moment, it disappears again.

9. Finally, we should look upon things in the spirit in which we watch the **clouds** on a hot summer day. They change their shape all the time, but as far as our welfare is concerned, one shape is as good as another. So do the transformations of the earthly scene not at all concern our true welfare.

9. THE SECOND CONCLUSION

32b. Thus spoke the Lord. Enraptured, the Elder Subhuti, the monks and nuns, the pious laymen and laywomen, and the Bodhisattvas, and the whole world with its Gods, men, Asuras and Gandharvas rejoiced in the Lord's teaching.

This is the traditional ending of a Mahayana Sutra.

The Frontispiece to the Tun Huang Print

A Chinese translation of the *Diamond Sutra* has the distinction of being the oldest printed book known to us. The printing of this roll, which is sixteen feet long, was completed by Wang Chieh on May 11, 868. It has survived because at a later period it was stored at Tun Huang in the Cave of the Thousand Buddhas, from where Sir Aurel Stein, about forty years ago, took it to the British Museum. Printing from wooden blocks was apparently invented early in the ninth century, and this is our earliest datable woodcut. Although it has a certain charm of its own, it is clearly an example of provincial art, and without that elegance and finish we associate with works executed in Lo-yang and other centres of T'ang culture.

In the centre we see the **Lord Buddha,** seated cross-legged on a lotus throne, expounding the 'Diamond Sutra'. His right hand is in the gesture of explaining or demonstrating the doctrine, while the left lies in his lap. The **Svastika** is one of the traditional 'marks' found on a Buddha's body, normally on the soles of his feet and the palms of his hands. Buddha-images show it only rarely on the chest. Where they do so, it signifies that it is not the historical Buddha who is represented, but his glorified body (technically known as *sambhoga-kāya*), the body in which he expounds the more profound, spiritual and esoteric teachings to those ready to hear them. The **third eye,** the eye of wisdom, also is noteworthy here, because it is not the usual simple circle, but shows the sun superimposed on the moon, a Tantric symbol.

Subhuti kneels on a mat in front of the Buddha, with his hands folded, and with his shoes, or slippers, by his side, in token of respect. To dispel any doubts about the identity of the figure, the cartouche at the lower left edge says in Chinese, 'Subhuti the Elder'. The woodcut illustrates the preamble to the

Diamond Sutra (chapter 2) where we hear that Subhuti 'rose from his seat, put his upper robe over one shoulder, placed his right knee on the earth, bent forth his folded hands towards the Lord, and said to him, etc.' And here we see Subhuti doing just that.

The glorified Buddha is held to sit on the 'Lion Throne', symbolized here by the **two lions** in front of the altar. If they look more like Pekinese dogs than like lions, this is not very surprising. The Pekinese dog, or 'Manchu-Lion-Dog' as it is called in Chinese, was bred in Peking to represent the lion of Mañjuśrī (Mon-ju), patron of the Man-chu dynasty. Since they had never seen a lion, the breeders had only the pictures of lions in Buddhist scrolls and paintings to go by, and we must admit that they achieved quite a good likeness to them. On the **altar** itself we can see an incense burner, as well as sacred vessels which contain pure water.

To the left and right of the Buddha two **demonic guardians** stand in warlike pose. The figure on the left brandishes a pike, or perhaps a thunderbolt, and he stands on lotuses (and not on tortoises, as one might think at first sight). The one on the right gesticulates with his clenched fists, and stands on lumps of rock. These two guardians of the Dharma, called 'the two generals Heng and Ha', developed in China from various antecedents in Indian Buddhism. They have the function to protect the preaching of the Dharma from interference by demons and other malevolent forces.

Now to the background. The Chinese inscription at the top left corner tells us that the scene depicted is the **'Garden of Anathapindika'**, in agreement with chapter 1 of the *Diamond Sutra*. The floor is paved with square tiles ornamented with a floral design. I personally am inclined to believe that these tiles represent the 'chequer-board pattern' which the Scriptures ascribe to a 'Pure Land', but experts have assured me that this is not so. Overhead we see flowering boughs, and a **canopy** with richly decorated tassels. It was usual in India to erect such canopies above royal personages or greatly revered spiritual teachers.

The **audience** of the *Diamond Sutra* comprises, according to chapter 32*b*, 'the monks and nuns, the pious laymen and laywomen, the Bodhisattvas, and the whole world with its Gods, men, Asuras and Gandharvas'. Ten **monks and nuns,** recognizable by their shaven heads, are shown in our picture. Two **Bodhisattvas** are marked by their crowns and haloes. A Bodhisattva wears the crown of a king because he is 'a great being' (see p. 23), a princely, magnificent emissary from the shining realms of the spirit. Ordinary monks are in this Mahayana Scripture regarded as inferior to the Bodhisattvas. They are, even including Subhuti, shown not only without crowns, but even without haloes. In the lower right-hand corner we have five **laymen and laywomen**—a Chinese dignitary in official robes and head-dress, with two men and two boys (or, ?women) in attendance on him. This leaves the Devas, Asuras and Gandharvas. The Asuras, who in any case are rather quarrelsome and unpleasant people, are not shown anywhere. But, above in the sky, we can discern two **angels** floating in the clouds, offering, in homage to the Buddha, flowers and fruit on a dish. One of them is a Deva, or God, and the other a Gandharva, or celestial nymph.

All the more important details are now, I think, accounted for. The Chinese writing to the left of the woodcut is, incidentally, not the beginning of the Sutra itself, but a kind of Preface, which says: 'If you want to recite this Sutra, you must first recite the following mantra, so as to purify your mouth, i.e. Tun-li tun-li, mahā-tunli, tun-tun-li, svāhā.' And so on.

The Heart Sutra

Sanskrit text,
Translation and Commentary

I. THE INVOCATION[1]

Oṃ namo Bhagavatyai Ārya-Prajñāpāramitāyai!

[1]Homage to the Perfection of Wisdom, the Lovely, the Holy!

The word *Bhagavatī*, which I have rendered as **Lovely**, can also be translated as 'Lady'. *Ārya* is not only **'Holy'**, but also 'noble', and is an attribute of the Buddhas and of those of their disciples who have definitely turned away from this world to the world of the spirit. (See p. 38.) It is difficult to say about this invocation much that is of use to the general reader. Its repetition should help us to raise our minds in reverence to the perfection of wisdom, as the mother of the Buddhas, as our guide through the world, and as the embodiment of perfect purity. Devotion may be strengthened by the contemplation of images, and by recalling the thirty-two epithets of wisdom (*BT* nos. 37 and 141) or Rahulabhadra's *Hymn to Perfect Wisdom* (*BT* no. 142). These matters must be left to oral instruction.

II. THE PROLOGUE

Ārya-Avalokiteśvaro bodhisattvo gambhīrāṃ prajñāpāramitā-caryāṃ caramāṇo vyavalokayati sma: pañca-skandhās tāṃś ca svabhāvaśūnyān paśyati sma.

[2]Avalokita, [3]The Holy Lord and Bodhisattva, [4]was moving in the deep course [5]of the Wisdom which has gone beyond. [6]He looked down from on high, [7]He beheld but five

---

[1] On the translated text of this Sutra I have superimposed a framework of Arabic numbers, sixty-one of them, to facilitate cross-references. Each of the eight sub-sections is again numbered with Roman numbers, and provided with a heading which is printed in capital letters.

heaps, ⁸and he saw that in their own-being they were empty.

Avalokiteśvara is called **Avalokita** because he 'looks down' (also no. 6) compassionately on this world. He is called **Holy** because he is one of the saints who have won the spiritual Path. He is called **Lord** (*īśvara*) because he has sovereignty over the world and power to help suffering beings, as for instance explained in the famous twenty-fourth chapter of the *Lotus of the Good Law*. And he is also called a **Bodhisattva:** a Bodhi-sattva (literally: Enlightenment-being) is an enlightened being who is on the way to becoming a Buddha, but who has postponed his entrance into Nirvana, and his escape from this world of birth-and-death, for the purpose of helping suffering creatures. In other words, a Bodhisattva is a being (*sattva*) who strives for enlightenment, and who cares for nothing but enlightenment. Alternatively, his essence (*sattva*) is enlightenment, i.e. in him the urge for the enlightenment of a Buddha replaces the will to live which keeps most of us going.

The phrase **was moving in the deep course** represents an attempt to reproduce the Sanskrit as literally as possible. It means that he 'was engaged in the practice' of perfect wisdom. **The wisdom which has gone beyond** is a literal rendering of *prajñāpāramitā: prajñā* = wisdom, *pāram* = beyond, *itā* = she who has gone. One could also speak of 'transcendental' wisdom. This wisdom has gone beyond everything earthly, or sensory, and yet, as we shall see, it has left none of it behind.

This first sentence, in an indirect and slightly mythological way, indicates the authoritative experience from which the teaching of this Sutra is derived, as well as the level on which it may be attained. In his very person the Bodhisattva Avalokiteśvara embodies that fusion of the Conditioned and the Absolute, of the world and Emptiness, which is recommended in the later sections of this Sutra. In Avalokiteśvara the religious imagination of the Mahayana has created the ideal of a person who strives to win enlightenment, but who is unwilling to enter the bliss of emancipation unless he can take the whole of creation with him. Engaged in transcendental wisdom Avalokita would, by definition, contemplate emptiness. And since emptiness is the same as Nirvana and the same as the Buddha, it is said that he looks at the self-illuminating splendour of the emptiness of the Buddhas when he thus practises.

Since, however, in Avalokita wisdom is coupled with compassion, he does not become so entranced with and absorbed in the sight of the Buddhas that he forgets everything else. He is thought of as a being who had made the 'great Vow of a Bodhisattva', i.e. 'I shall not enter final Nirvana before all beings have been liberated'. By entering final Nirvana (mentioned in no. 44), the Bodhisattva would completely cut himself off from this world, and thereby abandon the beings in it to their fate. But:

'Can there be bliss when all that lives must suffer?
Shalt thou be saved and hear the whole world cry?'

From compassion Avalokita, without losing his grip over emptiness, **looked down from on high** on this world of suffering creatures.

We can now proceed to the second sentence: Although Avalokita is aware of the sufferings of beings, and suffers with them, making their pains his own, nevertheless, when he cast his glance at this swarming multitude of men, animals, ghosts and angels, all more or less ill at ease, he did not see any persons or beings at all. Where ignorance imagines a personality or a living being, wisdom beholds **but five heaps**. The Sanskrit for 'heaps' is skandhas. The skandhas are the five constituents of our personality as it appears. On analysis, all the data of our experience—of ourselves and of objects in relation to us—can be stated in terms of these skandhas, without introducing the nebulous word 'I'. Buddhaghosa says of them that they 'define the limits of the basis of grasping after a self, and what belongs to a self'. They occur again in no. 16 and 24, where they will be explained in greater detail. At present it is sufficient to bear in mind that the first step towards wisdom consists in getting the *skandhas* into view. This requires considerable knowledge, practice and skill, but it is the indispensable basis for all that follows.

When this had been achieved, Avalokita **saw that in their own-being they were empty.** He **saw**: It is the special function of wisdom to penetrate into the own-being of things. Avalokita saw into it directly with his 'wisdom eye'. This wisdom eye, to quote Buddhaghosa again, 'has Nirvana for its object, and it has removed the latent tendencies towards ignorance'.

As for the terms 'own-being' and 'empty', they condense in fourteen Sanskrit letters the results of centuries of meditation, which cannot be adequately communicated in a few lines. That much, however, may be said about the meaning of the words: To see events in their **own-being** is the same as to see them as they really are in themselves. Their real nature is normally overclouded (see nos. 40 and 41) by the appearance they present to us under the influence of greed, aggressiveness and delusion. Since all greed, etc., is bound up with the illusion of selfhood, the concept of 'dharmas as they really are themselves' is, from the very start, contrasted with 'things and persons as seen with reference to a self'. In other words, when Avalokita saw the skandhas in their own being, he saw a constant appearance and disappearance of mere dharmas (mentioned in no. 18), or impersonal events.

The second step towards wisdom therefore consists in getting *dharmas* into view.

And these dharmas Avalokita then saw as **empty.** I have written elsewhere (*B* pp. 130-1) about the etymological derivation of the word *śūnyatā* from the root 'swell', and about its meaning (*SS* pp. 19-24). There is no need to repeat all this here. It will be sufficient to briefly define 'emptiness' from three points of view:

1. *Etymologically*, śūnya conveys the idea that something, which looks like something much, is really nothing. From outside there appears to be a lot, but there is really nothing behind. A 'swelled' head, as we know, is an 'empty' head.

2. As a *spiritual* term, emptiness denotes the complete denial of, the complete liberation from, the world around us in all its aspects and along its entire breadth.

3. As a *technical* term it denotes in Buddhism the absence of any kind of self. First of all, all dharmas are 'empty' in the sense that in their reality no 'self' can be found, nothing that owns, nothing that belongs. Secondly, all dharmas are empty in

the sense that each one depends so much on others that it is nothing by or in itself. In the ultimate sense, dharmas do therefore not exist as separate entities. If taken quite by itself, as unconditioned, a dharma is the Void, and its own-being is emptiness.

These two sides of emptiness have been the subject of Buddhist meditation for a long time. The Theravadins and Sarvastivadins generally stress the first (i.e. the absence of a self, *ātman*), the Madhyamikas the second (i.e. the absence of an own-being, *svabhāva*).

Familiarity with *emptiness* is therefore the third preliminary step in the direction of Perfect Wisdom.

III. THE DIALECTICS OF EMPTINESS. FIRST STAGE

iha Śāriputra rūpaṁ śūnyatā śūnyataiva rūpaṁ, rūpān na prithak śūnyatā śūnyatāyā na prithag rūpaṁ, yad rūpaṁ sā śūnyatā yā śūnyatā tad rūpaṁ; evam eva vedanā-saṁjñā-saṁskāra-vijñānaṁ.

[9]Here, O Śāriputra, [10]form is emptiness and the very emptiness is form; [11]emptiness does not differ from form, [12]form does not differ from emptiness; [13]whatever is form, that is emptiness, [14]whatever is emptiness, that is form, [15]the same is true of [16]feelings, perceptions, impulses and consciousness.

Here means, on the level of compassionate transcendental wisdom. But why is it **Śāriputra** who is addressed here? Śāriputra (the son of Śārī) was among the eighty chief disciples of the Buddha Śākyamuni, the one noted for his wisdom. His influence on the development of Buddhist thought has been a decisive one, as I have shown elsewhere (*B* pp. 90–3). The 'wisdom' which is attributed to him is skill in the methods of the Abhidharma. Its chief feature is the analysis of experience into its constituent elements, called 'dharmas', in accordance with traditional lists of what are to be regarded as 'ultimate facts'. The teaching is addressed to Sariputra in order to indicate that it begins where the Abhidharma ends. Conversely, for any deeper understanding of this Sutra some preparatory training in Abhidharma methods is necessary. We can at this

point picture to ourselves the Venerable Sariputra, with his
shaven head and saffron robe, as he stands by the Buddha's side,
holds out his folded hands in reverence, and waits for instruction.

It is here assumed that Sariputra had taken the first step in
the understanding of emptiness, but that, like many other
Disciples of Gautama, he was inclined to stop there. It is
assumed, in other words, that Sariputra, when he lived at the
time of the Buddha Śākyamuni, was only at an inferior stage
of his discipline and progress; then only an Arhat, he will one
day become a Buddha. In the *Lotus of the Good Law* we actually
hear how the Buddha prophesied the future Buddhahood of
Sariputra (*BT* no. 122).

To lift Sariputra above himself, Avalokita now makes three
statements about the relation between each skandha and
emptiness. The five skandhas are enumerated in nos: 10 and 16:
form (*rūpa*) covers the 'material' or 'physical' aspect of the
world, and it comprises chiefly the four material elements, the
five sense organs and the five sense objects. **Feelings** are
pleasant, unpleasant or neutral. **Perceptions** are made through
the six senses—eye, ear, nose, tongue, body, mind (as nos.
25–6). **Impulses** is a none too satisfactory rendering of
samskāra, literally 'together-makers' (sam-s-kāra). The term
includes all active dispositions, tendencies, impulses, volitions,
strivings, etc., whether 'conscious' or 'repressed'. **Consciousness** is the awareness of something. It implies a
separation of subject and object, and a discrimination between
object and object. The prefix *vi-* in *vijñāna* expresses this
essentially discriminatory function.

These five skandhas constitute our 'personality'. They are also
co-extensive with the conditioned world, and we can treat
'conditioned events' as a synonym of 'the five skandhas'.

The language of section III presents no further difficulties to
the understanding. Its message, however, puts a considerable
strain on our thinking apparatus, because on the face of it just
plain nonsense is here propounded. In fact this is the true
Lion's Roar of the lion of the tribe of the Sakyas, and those who
have not fled out of earshot will now be told about it.

The identity of Nirvana and Samsara can be explained only
to those who have already understood it. It is, of course, quite

easy to see that in a way Nirvana and 'this world' are not the same. All one has to do is to pay attention to the meaning of the words, which mean two totally different things. Life in this world results from the loss of the peaceful calm of Nirvana, and Nirvana from the total rejection of this world. Nothing could be more obvious. We must, on the other hand, think very hard, and put a most unwelcome strain on our little grey cells, if we want to appreciate the opposite thesis, which identifies Nirvana and Samsara. At one stage of self-discipline it. is useful to differentiate Nirvana from this world. On another level of spiritual awareness Nirvana may reveal itself as the same as this world. The teaching of this Sutra sets out to describe the vision and insight of the perfect. It is bound to seem rather absurd to those who are not. To the spiritually blind it conveys, of course, nothing whatever, but to those who strive to win spiritual freedom it affords a glimpse, from afar, of the vision which awaits them at the end.

Self-denial is the essence of the spiritual life. As long as the self still struggles to extinguish itself in emptiness, it will set form against emptiness, and so on. But where self-extinction is accomplished, there a non-difference of world and emptiness will ensue. Since denial of self is itself an act of self, that denial, to be complete, has in its turn also to be denied. In this way a position may be spiritually sound, and yet absurd from the point of view of ordinary logic.

'Emptiness' is our word for the Beyond, for transcendental reality. That the transcendental is Beyond is self-evident. The corollary, that.it is also immanent, in its opposite, and co-exists with it, is taught even to children and ordinary people. But that it should be precisely identical with its exact opposite, or with that which it is not, that surely passes belief. And yet, that is the message of our section III. The infinitely Far-away is not only near, but it is *infinitely* near. It is nowhere, and nowhere it is not. This is the mystical identity of opposites. Nirvana is the same as the world. It is not only 'in' and 'with you', but you are nothing but it.

To stress the fact that the identity of Beyond and not-Beyond is not a partial but a total one, three formulations are here used: no. 10 postulates an absolute, complete and reciprocal identity; nos. 11–12 the absence of any kind of difference, both in their extent and their content; and according to nos. 13–14 their abstract concepts coincide, as well as the concrete events to which they may apply. Professor Murti has lucidly summed up the Madhyamika position on this question: 'There is no difference whatever between Nirvana and Samsara; Noumenon and Phenomena are not two separate sets of entities, nor are they two states of the same thing. The absolute looked at through the thought-forms of constructive imagination is the empirical world; and conversely, the absolute is the world viewed *sub specie aeternitatis*, without the distorting media of Thought.'[1]

It is not the function of a commentary to render this paradoxical doctrine plausible, to guard it against misunderstandings, or to show up its manifold theoretical, spiritual and practical consequences. A few words about its *logical* implications are, however, quite unavoidable: 'Emptiness' is a state which results from complete self-denial, and from the renunciation of all things. By its very definition it is the negation of the skandhas. One term (i.e. the skandhas) is here therefore deliberately identified with what was defined as its negation and complete denial. In logical parlance, 'A is what A is not', or 'what A is not, that is A'. Such propositions obviously violate the logical principle of contradiction. For to identify a term with its negation is to state a contradiction. The identity of Yes and No is the secret of emptiness. No. 10 asserts that 'form is the denial of form, and the very denial of form is form'. Or, in other words, the asserting of A, is the denying of A, and the very denying of A is the asserting of A. In this way logic defeats itself. Logical asserting and denying cannot be regarded as ultimately valid operations where true reality is concerned. Aristotle pointed out in his 'Metaphysics' that the rejection of the principle of contradiction must lead to the conclusion that 'all things are one'. This seemed to him manifestly absurd. Here, conversely, the insight into the oneness of all is the great goal, and only by contradictions can it be attained.

'Dialectics' is the technical term for a method which deliberately abrogates the principle of contradiction. Section III establishes what may be called a 'dialectical' conception of emptiness. The emptiness which is envisaged here is not empty

[1] *The Central Philosophy of Buddhism*, 1955, p. 274.

of that which it excludes, but it includes it, is identical with it, is full of it. It is therefore a 'Full Emptiness' which we have obtained as a result of section III. Its implications are now unfolded in IV and V.

IV. THE DIALECTICS OF EMPTINESS. SECOND STAGE

Iha Śāriputra sarva-dharmāḥ śūnyatā-lakṣaṇā, anutpannā aniruddhā, amalā avimalā, anūnā aparipūrṇāḥ.

[17]Here, O Sariputra, [18]all dharmas are marked with emptiness; [19]they are not produced or stopped, [20]not defiled or immaculate, [21]not deficient or complete.

The progress of the argument is indicated by the change in the grammatical subject. Where section III dealt with the five skandhas, we now make a statement about all Dharmas. 'All dharmas' comprises not only the five skandhas, which are conditioned, but in addition also the unconditioned dharmas. The word 'all' may be taken either distributively or collectively, in other words, it may mean 'each one', 'any one', or 'all of them taken together'. 'Dharma' is a technical term for the events, happenings or facts which an analysis based on the conventions of the Abhidharma reveals as ultimately real. Sarvadharmāḥ should not be translated as 'all things'. A chair, a leaf, a sewer, a cuckoo are 'things', but not one of them is a 'dharma'. At some time or another most Buddhist schools drew up a list of factors which they regarded as 'dharmas'. In essentials all these lists agree. The Prajñāpāramitā texts work with the Abhidharma of the Sarvastivadins, who counted seventy-five ultimates. Their division is roughly as follows:

Unconditioned Dharmas

Space No. 1   Two kinds of Nirvana Nos. 2-3

Conditioned Dharmas

I. Form	II. Thought	III. Mentals	IV. Various
4-14	15	16-61	62-75

Under 'mentals' we have such dharmas as mindfulness, vigour, envy, and so on. Class IV includes 'attainment' (No. 62), 'non-attainment' (No. 63), both mentioned later in this Sutra, 'life-force' (No. 65) impermanence (No. 69), and so on. I am afraid that all this lore must here be taken for granted. Those who know French, can find the information in de la Vallée-Poussin's translation of Vasubandhu's *Abhidharmakośa*. In English we only have W. McGovern's *Manual of Buddhist Philosophy* (I, 1923), which is at least better than nothing.

Section III denied the difference and separateness of conditioned and unconditioned events. All dharmas have then one feature in common—they are all equally **marked with emptiness.** The Unconditioned is emptiness by definition, and the conditioned by the express identification effected in Section III. This emptiness is now said to be the essential and exclusive mark of all dharmas. In this one attribute all the other marks which Abhidharma tradition had considered, are swallowed up and become extinct. Some reflection will show that 'to be marked with emptiness' is the same as 'to be empty of all differentiating marks'. Dharmas are empty of all that could mark off a separate existence for each one of them, i.e. they have no separate existence. And as this is their one and only characteristic, and there is no other, one can say that it is their mark not only to be 'empty', but to be 'emptiness' itself. This mark should now be attended to, and, if this is done, its meaning unfolds itself from three points of view.

Nos. 19–21 derive their force from the tacit opposition to the Abhidharma doctrine, which attributed to the things of this world three universal, or general, marks. They are impermanence, suffering, lack of self. At this point we must bear in mind some of the assumptions concerning the Three Marks current among Abhidharmists, for it is their terminology which is here being used. They believed, as the following table shows, that some dharmas are produced and others stopped, some defiled and others immaculate, some deficient and others complete.

1. Every conditioned dharma is first produced and then it stops again. The contemplation of impermanence, of the 'rise and fall' of dharmas, formed an essential part of the monk's meditational training. By contrast, Nirvana, also known as The Permanent, The Eternal, The Unchangeable, is the state

where all conditioned events have definitely stopped. The Scriptures therefore often call it by the name of 'Stopping' (*nirodha*).

2. The relation of no. 20 to the second mark is less immediately obvious. Things are 'ill' because and in so far as they are connected with craving, and with the three 'taints' (*mala*), i.e. greed, hatred and delusion, which are also called 'defilements' (*kleśa*). The range of what is 'ill' therefore coincides with the range of what is 'defiled'. By contrast, Nirvana, in its blissful purity, is free from these taints, and can therefore be called the 'Undefiled', or the 'Immaculate'.

The Marks	This World = The Conditioned = The Relative = The five skandhas = Samsara	The Beyond = The Unconditioned = the Absolute = Emptiness = Nirvana
1. Impermanence	Both produced and stopped	Stopping
2. Ill	Defiled	Immaculate
3. Not-self (a) absence of a personal ego	—	—
(b) absence of an own-being	Incomplete	Complete

So far the 'wisdom' of the Abhidharma. The 'transcendental wisdom' of the Hridaya has, however, gone beyond the opposition between the conditioned and the unconditioned dharmas. If, as we saw, in fact these two classes are essentially the same, then they also do not differ in their marks. They are thus both equally **not produced or stopped, not defiled or immaculate.**

3. The reference to the third mark is more indirect and obscure. It is not easy to speak about 'not-self' without being smothered in verbal ambiguities. The Mahayana, as we said above (to no. 8), distinguishes two kinds of 'not-self' (*nairātmya*), the *pudgala-nairātmya* and the *dharma-nairātmya*. The first states that a personal ego (*ātman*) does not form a part of real

events as they actually are. The Abhidharma regarded this mark of not-self, unlike impermanence and ill, as common to conditioned and unconditioned dharmas alike. The attentive reader of the *Dhammapada* will notice that vv. 277–8 first state that 'all conditioned things (*sankhārā*) are impermanent and ill'. Verse 279 then adds, 'all *dharmas* are not-self'.

The Abhidharmists attempted to exorcise the illusory belief in a personal ego by a rigid meditational discipline which taught them to view all experience as an interplay of impersonal and momentary dharmas. Although a dharma is devoid of a personal ego, and has no reference to one, nevertheless in their system each dharma, to be what it is, is *itself*, and not something else. Each dharma possesses some attribute of its own, which defines its essential nature in its difference from others. In this way, the element of fire is defined by 'heat', consciousness is that 'which is aware of' something, and ignorance is 'lack of cognition'. Now, if a dharma is 'itself' because it has a certain number of properties essential to it, it must then automatically exclude from itself countless other facets of reality, which are either incompatible or just different. Fire would not be 'itself' if it were also cold and wet. Each one dharma is something apart (*pṛthak*, as at nos. 11–12) from all the other seventy-four dharmas. In the words of Spinoza, 'all determination involves a negation'. In order to be something definite, each dharma must exclude the greater part of reality from itself. Everything finite is therefore 'incomplete', or 'deficient', in the sense that it is deprived of all that lies outside its own particular nature as defined by its marks. By contrast the unconditioned is 'complete', is the all-embracing reality. Nothing that is anything is excluded from it. As finite things are on all sides hedged in and constrained by their properties and conditions, so Nirvana is the unconditioned fullness of reality and complete unrestricted freedom.

It is, however, clear that this opposition between deficiency and completeness arises only from the gratuitous introduction of the idea of a separate selfhood for different dharmas. Without it we would have just one emptiness, which would be **not deficient and not complete.** As we read in 'On Believing in Mind':

'In the higher realms of true Suchness
There is neither self nor other.
When direct identification is sought,
We can only say, Not two.
One in All,
All in One,—
If only this is realised,
No more worry about your not being perfect'.

V. THE DIALECTICS OF EMPTINESS. THIRD STAGE

Tasmāc Chāriputra śūnyatāyāṃ na rūpaṃ na vedanā na
saṃjñā na saṃskārāḥ na vijñānam. na cakṣuḥ-śrotra-ghrāṇa-
jihvā-kāya-manāṃsi. na rūpa-śabda-gandha-rasa-spraṣṭavya-
dharmāḥ. na cakṣur-dhātur yāvan na manovjñāna-dhātuḥ.
na-avidyā na-avidyā-kṣayo yāvan na jarā-maraṇaṃ na jarā-
maraṇa-kṣayo. na duḥkha-samudaya-nirodha-mārgā. na
jñānam, na prāptir na-aprāptiḥ.

[22]Therefore, O Śāriputra, [23]in emptiness [24]there is no
form, nor feeling, nor perception, nor impulse, nor
consciousness; [25]No eye, ear, nose, tongue, body, mind;
[26]No forms, sounds, smells, tastes, touchables or objects
of mind; [27]No sight-organ element, [28]and so forth, until
we come to: [29]No mind-consciousness element; [30]There
is no ignorance, [31]no extinction of ignorance, [32]and so
forth, until we come to: [33]there is no decay and death, no
extinction of decay and death. [34]There is no suffering, no
origination, no stopping, no path. [35]There is no cognition,
[36]no attainment and no non-attainment.

The 'Full Emptiness', obtained in Section III, was in IV
shown to be all-comprehensive. Section V now completes the
dialectical circle, and again denies the initial assertion of
Section III. **Therefore,** i.e. because all dharmas are nothing
but emptiness, **in emptiness,** or 'where there is emptiness',
there all these dharmas are not. We must bear in mind that here
nothing but ignorance (itself a negation, *a-vidyā*) is excluded
from the Absolute. Those whose views are entirely derived
from ignorance will naturally fear to be left with nothing at all.
Not so those in whom the eye of wisdom is open, for they know

that only those things are denied here which obstruct its vision. In no. 40 they recur under the name of 'thought-coverings'.

The reader must, however, be warned that the words in nos. 22–24 do not mean what they say. The word **Therefore,** to begin with, draws a conclusion, and it occurs three times in this Sutra (nos. 22, 37, 50). In each case it indicates a conclusion which is not immediately obvious (as at 50), paradoxical (because 37 is contradicted by 44), and invalid by the rules of ordinary logic (as in this case, since it brings no. 24 into contradiction with no. 14). The **in** can obviously have no spatial meaning. Nor can the **is,**—implied by the Sanskrit, and stated in the English—be an ordinary 'is', because it is equivalent to 'is not', the duality of 'is' and 'is not' having been abolished or transcended. And the **not** also cannot be an ordinary 'not', because it is used in a proposition of which one term, i.e. 'emptiness', is itself a self-contradictory unity of Yes and No. The Sanskrit *na* is rendered by *wu(mu)* in the Chinese, which in its turn is the answer to the famous *koan*, 'Is the Buddha-nature in this dog?'

Molière, the playwright, had a cook without whose approval none of his works was ever passed for publication. Similarly, I always submit my manuscripts to one or two persons who, in their capacity as 'average Westerners', guide me in my attempts to make the Wisdom of the East intelligible to Europeans. These mentors of mine could follow fairly well up to now, but when they were faced with the third somersault of the Dialectics, their heads began to reel. I had written that 'in a logic which identifies Yes and No, it is only logical that the identity of world and emptiness should lead to their complete separateness'. This to me self-evident statement seemed to have no meaning for them at all. I had explained that 'an absolute identity (as in section III) is the same as an absolute difference (as in section V); because a relation between the Absolute and anything else is an "absolute relation", a contradiction in terms, and quite different in its behaviour from what is usually called a "relation".' But my friends only sadly shook their heads, and wearily rubbed their eyes, as if dazed by so much splendour. So I have decided that one ought not to be too ambitious in one's efforts to make the implausible plausible. Suffice it to say that the Emptiness which, according to III, contains all the manifold multiplicity of the world, is, as the One, as well empty of anything that has been counted as a separate dharma, whether conditioned or unconditioned.

For the items enumerated in nos. 24–36 are, of course, equivalent to the 'all dharmas' of no. 18. The Sutra reproduces here an old, unsystematic, classification of 'all dharmas', which arranged them in five numerical lists, i.e. the five skandhas, the twelve sense-fields, the eighteen elements, the twelve links of conditioned co-production, and the four holy truths. The *Visuddhimagga*, in chapters 14–16, deals with them in just this order, and according to Buddhaghosa their knowledge forms the 'foundation' (*bhūmi*) of wisdom.

What then is here denied are (1) *the five skandhas*, (2) *the six sense-organs*, and (3) *the six sense-objects*. With regard to the latter (no. 26) we may note that **forms** here are the objects of sight. The term **touchables** includes not only the objects of touch proper, but also the objects of the temperature sense, the kinaesthetic sense, the sense of balance, and the somatic sense by which we perceive the inward condition of our body, in hunger, thirst, fatigue, etc. **Objects of mind** are those parts of the world which we perceive through the sixth sense-organ, i.e. feelings, perceptions, impulses, the subtle forms of matter, and unconditioned things (space and, in a way, Nirvana). Next, (4) we come to the *eighteen elements* of all our experience. They are the six sense-organs (as in no. 25), the six sense-objects (as in no. 26), and the six corresponding kinds of consciousness. The phrase **and so forth, until we come to,** is a stylistic device constantly used in these Sutras for stereotyped lists presumed to be familiar. All it means is that one should mentally supplement the enumeration which is here abbreviated.

As item 5 we have the *twelve links* of the chain of causation, i.e. **ignorance,** formative forces, consciousness, name-and-form, the (12) sense-fields, contact, feeling, craving, grasping, becoming, birth, **decay and death.** The traditional formula (as e.g. *BT* no. 41) recites first the order of their production from one another, and thereafter their successive **extinction.**

Item 6 refers to the *four holy Truths,* i.e. (1) Individual separate existence is inevitably bound up with **suffering,** or ill; (2) suffering has its **origination** from craving; (3) There is a

stopping of ill when craving has ceased; (4) The eightfold **path** leads to the cessation of ill. No. 34 sums up the entire *Hridaya*, and provides the clue for its understanding. The 'Heart Sutra', as a matter of fact, has been planned out as a restatement of the four holy Truths. Some subtlety of mind is needed to see the connections, and I leave my readers to ponder the issue for themselves. My own answer must be postponed until the end of section VII.

Then (7) **No cognition.** 'Cognition', or 'gnosis', *jñāna*, is the understanding, by the wise, of the categories mentioned in nos. 24 to 34, and of their bearing on all the phenomena of experience. Since everything which constitutes the object of emancipating cognition is absent in emptiness, how can that cognition itself be present in it?

Finally, (8) **Attainment** means the obtaining of ecstatic meditation, of the four Paths (of a Streamwinner, Once-Returner, Never-Returner, and Arhat), and of the enlightenment of Buddhahood.

To show the connection of V with the preceding argument of IV, I will indicate how these eight items can be grouped into conditioned and unconditioned events. We know from the *Vibhanga*,[1] and other sources, that this kind of grouping was a favourite exercise of Buddhist monks.

Conditioned Events	*Unconditioned Events*
1. Five skandhas	
2, 3. Eleven sense-fields, and part of twelfth.	part of twelfth, i.e. of the sense-field of mind-objects (dharmas)
4. Seventeen elements, and part of the eighteenth	part of the eighteenth, i.e. of the element of mind-objects
5. Ignorance, up to: decay and death	extinction of ignorance, up to: extinction of decay and death
6. First, second and fourth Truth	third Truth
7. Cognition	
8. Attainment	

[1] Pp. 64, 75, 93, 116.

VI. THE CONCRETE EMBODIMENT OF FULL EMPTINESS,
AND ITS PRACTICAL BASIS

Tasmāc Chāriputra aprāptitvād bodhisattvasya prajñāpāra-
mitām āśritya viharaty acittāvaraṇaḥ. cittāvaraṇa-nāstitvād
atrasto viparyāsa-atikrānto nishṭhā-nirvāṇa-prāptaḥ.

[37]Therefore, O Sariputra, it is because of his non-
attainmentness that [38]a Bodhisattva, [39]through having
relied on the perfection of wisdom, [40]dwells without
thought-coverings. [41]In the absence of thought-coverings
[42]he has not been made to tremble, [43]he has overcome
what can upset, [44]and in the end he attains to Nirvana.

Having so far considered the nature of reality, we now turn
to the persons who strive to win salvation in it. The dialectical
concept of Emptiness, as explained in sections III to V, is
now related to the concrete career and mode of living of those
heroic beings whose lives are dominated by enlightenment, and
who are known first as Bodhisattvas, and then as Buddhas. As
long as it is treated in abstraction from the Path which leads to
its experience, emptiness has been explained only very imperfectly. Section VI now describes the spiritual conditions
under which it may be realized, and hints at the stages of their
fulfilment. Before I explain the terms one by one, I will first
sum up its contents so as to bring out the progressive development:

1. Full Emptiness presupposes three spiritual conditions:
(a) It is attained by a non-attainmentness (no. 37), (b) carried
out by a Bodhisattva (as against an Arhat who is content with
personal Nirvana) (no. 38), (c) who has relied on nothing but
the emptiness revealed by transcendental wisdom (no. 39).

2. It is realized in three steps (nos. 40-3), each of which
eliminates a dualism: (a) The dualism between the Bodhisattva's
Thought and its objects is denied. In consequence of the act of
total renunciation implied in (1c) he dwells without the separate
and multiple thoughts (which were denied already in nos.
24-37) (no. 40). (b) The dualism between the Bodhisattva (as a
subject) and the absence of thought-coverings (as a kind of
object) is removed, and therefore all possibility of his trembling,
or of being shaken out of his career (nos. 41, 42). (c) All difference

between the three Marks and their opposites is ignored. Nothing thus can possibly upset (no. 43).

3. The Bodhisattva's non-attainmentness then miraculously leads to the attainment of Nirvana (no. 44).

Now to the terms used. **Non-attainmentness** sums up the 'no attainment and no non-attainment' of no. 36, which in their turn summarized section V. It can be understood to mean that the Bodhisattva is 'indifferent to any kind of personal attainment', and so I have translated in *BT* 146 and *SS* 54. Using an old English mystical term one can also say that the Bodhisattva is 'devoid of any propriety'.

The subject of the sentence is **a Bodhisattva,** or 'the Bodhisattva'. The developed concept of Full Emptiness has no meaning by itself, or for those who are animated by the ideal of Arhatship and personal Nirvana (see *SS* nos. 5–7), but only for the Bodhisattvas, who had in no. 3 been exemplified by Avalokiteśvara.

Through having relied on nothing but **the perfection of wisdom.** This phrase restates the practical meaning of the attitude by which emptiness was gained. What one had to do was not to rely on anything, worldly or otherwise, to let it all go, to give the resulting emptiness a free run, unobstructed by anything whatever, or by the fight against it. To stop relying on anything, to seek nowhere any refuge or support, that is to be supported by 'the perfection of wisdom'. The Perfection of Wisdom can, of course, be equated with Emptiness, and so at this stage the Bodhisattva relies on nothing but emptiness. He is able to bear the absolute aloneness of his solitary Spirit. Our separate self is a spurious reality, which can maintain itself only by finding supports, or props, on which to lean, or rely (see *B* 22–3). This tendency is rooted in the very fibres of our being. The kind of mental life which springs from ignorance seeks for ever to build a fictitious security on what is in fact quite unstable and untrustworthy.

To go for refuge to the Three Treasures is the central act of the Buddhist religion. It is its central insight that 'neither heaven nor earth are my shelter', that a safe refuge is to be found nowhere at all. This idea is also expressed in Matthew viii.

20, where the Son of Man is said to have nowhere where he could lay his head.

He dwells: The term 'dwells' is used in the Buddhist Scriptures for a firm, settled, well-established mode of behaviour. Although he has only emptiness to hold on to, the Bodhisattva does not just tumble headlong into an abyss, but somehow he still remains stable and settled in the emptiness.

Without thought-coverings: The Sanskrit compound, *a-citta-āvaraṇaḥ*, is a fine example of manifold meanings packed into one short formula. *A-* is, of course, 'not', 'without'. *Citta* is either (*a*) 'thoughts', mental activities, or (*b*) 'Thought', Spirit. *Āvaraṇa*, from the root *vṛi* (see also no. 44), means 'obstruction', 'obstacle', 'impediment', 'covering'. Buddhist tradition normally distinguishes three kinds of impediment—practical, moral and cognitive. They are (1) the *karma-āvaraṇa*, which are the obstacles to spiritual development that arise from those wrong deeds of the past which must still be expiated, and force us to live in an unfavourable and inauspicious environment; (2) the *kleśa-āvaraṇa*, the obstacles arising from the defilements, such as greed, hate and so on; (3) the *jñeya-āvaraṇa*, literally 'the obstruction from what is cognizable', which are the impediments arising from the belief in the real existence of separate objects. The term used here, *citta-āvaraṇa*, is very rare, and I assume it to be identical with the third kind of obstacles, the cognitive ones. Some manuscripts of the Hridaya read 'Thought-object' (*citta-ālambana*) instead.

The series of negations, which make up section V, does not add up to nothingness, but points the way to a unique ultimate reality. This has so far been called 'emptiness', and it is found by Perfect Wisdom in an identity of subject and object.

'In one Emptiness the two are not distinguished,
And each contains in itself all the ten thousand things'.[1]

Where this ineffable Oneness is spoken of, it may either be described as an object without a subject, or as a subject without an object. When viewed as an object without a subject, it is

---

[1] *On Believing in Mind*, v. 14. The 'two' are here subject and object, as the context shows quite clearly.

called 'Suchness'. When viewed from the subject-side, the transcendental reality is known as 'Thought-only', because, one and simple, free from duality and multiplicity, it is without a separate object. This Thought, or Spirit, forms the very centre of our being. Chuang Tse had a similar conception when he said:

'The work of the Ear ends with Hearing;
The work of the Mind ends with Ideas.
But the Spirit is an emptiness ready to take in all things'.

Usually, this absolute Thought is, however, obscured by the thoughts, or mental activities, of our surface mind. 'Thought-coverings' is just another term for 'ignorance', for the 'delusion' which all along had been held by Buddhist tradition to cover up the true nature of dharmic facts and to hide it from us. Ignorance throws over reality a veil of manufactured entities, all of which somehow contain the false idea of 'self', overclouding with their multiplicity the essential oneness of Nirvana. It is, on the other hand, the task of wisdom 'to disperse the darkness of illusion which covers up the own-being of dharmas',[1] and to dis-cover what they really are.

To the Spirit in us all external and internal objects—imaginary, false, sham supports—are obstacles, obstructions to vision, impediments to the free flow of transcendental wisdom. Our eyes blind, our ears deafen, our intellects stupefy us. Thoughts about anything that may fall under the skandhas, sensefields, and so on, must cease for Thought itself to find itself again. Whatever seems to feed that Thought really chokes and hinders it. To get Thought alone, purely by itself—then one is 'without thought-coverings', emancipated in the supreme glory of a thought which refers to nothing definite at all, and also leads to nowhere in particular.

In the absence of thought-coverings: The Bodhisattva, finding himself all alone, faced with the absence of all thoughts, will, as long as he distinguishes himself from that state, be exposed to the anxiety which comes from the loss of support. As it is said in the *Abhidharmakośa* (II 43c): 'The ordinary person cannot produce the highest trance, in which both

[1] *Visuddhimagga*, p. 438.

perception and feeling are stopped, because he is frightened of annihilation'. Similarly the *Prajñāpāramitā Sutras* often discuss the anxiety which would result from their false nihilistic interpretation. Nos. 41–2 now deal with that difficulty. It is capable of two successive interpretations: (1) *In spite of* the absence of multiple thoughts there is no trembling, once the Bodhisattva and the absence of multiple thoughts are seen as non-different. (2) When this is done, the last vestige of multiplicity disappears, and *because of* the absence of thought-coverings trembling ceases. For there is nothing left to tremble at, nor can there be the anxiety of a cut-off separate being who might quite well go on trembling even after there is nothing left to tremble about.

That can upset: The Sanskrit is *vi-pary-āsa*, often translated as 'perverted views'. This does not affect the meaning, because we can never be upset by any fact, but only by our wrong interpretation of it, i.e. when we try to make things do what is not in them to do. Traditionally there are four 'perverted views', which cover all attempts to seek, or to find, (1) permanence, (2) ease, (3) selfhood, and (4) delight, in that which is essentially (1) impermanent, (2) inseparable from suffering, (3) not linked to any self, and (4) repulsive or unlovely. Akin to ignorance, the root evil, they can be viewed as mis-searches (looking for permanence, etc., in the wrong place), or mis-takes, or reversals (of the truth), or as over-throwers of inner calm. Perverted views are on this level not merely rejected, but completely **overcome,** or 'stepped above' (*atikrāmati*), when no longer any difference is seen between permanence and impermanence, ease and ill, self and not-self, delight and disgust.

And in the end he attains to Nirvana.[1] Many Buddhist authors have derived the word 'Nirvana' from the root *vṛi*, 'to cover', interpreting it as that which is quite 'unobstructed', or 'free'. Nirvana is therefore here envisaged as the final stage of the removal of all obstructions, of the uncovering process, which formed the theme of nos. 40–1.

No. 44 obviously contradicts nos. 36 and 37. It is just because

---

[1] The translation differs here from *BT* and *SS*, where I give 'in the end sustained by Nirvana'. The manuscript tradition is uncertain at this point, and in *BT* and *SS* I have followed one reading, and here another.

he seeks no attainment, it is just because attainment is quite impossible, that the Bodhisattva attains, or wins, Nirvana. And entrance into Nirvana changes him into a Buddha.

VII. FULL EMPTINESS IS THE BASIS ALSO OF BUDDHAHOOD

tryadhva-vyavasthitāḥ   sarva-buddhāḥ   prajñāpāramitām-āśritya-anuttarāṃ samyaksambodhim abhisambuddhāḥ.

[45]All those who appear as Buddhas [46]in the three periods of time [47]fully awake to the [48]utmost, right and perfect enlightenment [49]because they have relied on the perfection of wisdom.

Not only the Bodhisattvas, but also **all the Buddhas** owe the attainment of their goal to the realization of the Full Emptiness of sections III to V. The Buddhas are countless, and **appear** in the different world-systems (see *B* p. 50), and in **the three periods of time,** i.e. the past, present and future. In order to win **enlightenment,** they had to cast everything aside, and to **rely** only **on the perfection of wisdom,** who is their mother (*SS* nos. 101–4), and on the emptiness perceived in that wisdom. The English language can do no justice to this sentence. In Sanskrit the words translated as 'Buddhas', 'awake' and 'enlightenment' all go back to the same root *budh* which in this Sutra forms the following five words: (1) *Buddhāḥ,* 'Buddhas' (no. 45), (2) *abhisambuddhāḥ,* 'have fully awoken' (no. 49), (3) *bodhi,* 'awakening' (no. 60), (4) *sambodhi,* 'perfect enlightenment' (no. 48), and (5) *bodhi-sattva,* 'Bodhisattva' (nos. 3, 38). Translated into English on the same pattern, these words would be, (1) 'the Enlightened Ones', (2) 'have been fully enlightened', (3) 'enlightenment', (4) 'perfect enlighten-ment', (5) 'enlightenment-being'. This sounds rather awkward, and still does no justice to the fact that the root *budh* combines a number of ideas which in no other language seem to coincide in one word. In English it may have the following five more or less distinct meanings: (*a*) *To awake,* i.e. to wake oneself up, to awaken others, to be awake or wakeful. As such it is opposed to being asleep, in the slumber of delusion, from which the enlightened awakens as from a dream. (*b*) *To recognize* as, to become aware of, acquainted with, to notice, give heed to—and so a Buddha is one who has recognized the evils of the defilements and has his eyes opened to a higher life. (c) *To know*, to understand. The Buddhas, free from all ignorance, know all the dharmas, they have completely understood all the four Truths, and the four Paths (or ways of spiritual development). (d) *To be enlightened*, to enlighten (as in il-lumin-ation). The opposite here is darkness, and the corresponding blindness of ignorance. (e) *To fathom*, a depth, or to penetrate, i.e. the obstructions, or coverings, discussed at no. 41.

It is rather striking that in this Sutra about one-fourth of the words with verbal roots are derived from roots expressing intellectual activity.

Jñā is at the basis of (1) *jñānam*, 'cognition' (no. 35), (2) *jñā-tavyam*, 'one should know' (no. 50), (3) *pra-jñā*, 'wisdom', (4) *sam-jñā*, 'perception' (16, 24), and (5) *vi-jñā-nam*, 'consciousness' (16, 24, 29). More literally, translated on the same pattern, the five words would be, (1) 'cognition' (the etymological equivalent), (2) 'one should cognize', (3) 'higher cognition', (4) 'co-cognition', (5) 'dis-cognition'. Other such roots are *vid* (at 16, 24; 30, 31; 53), *man* (at 25, 29, 52 sq.), and *cit* (at 40, 41). This Sutra is not meant for the stupid, the emotional, or the uninformed. Other means will assure their salvation. Everything that is at all worth knowing is contained in the *Hridaya*. But it can be found there only if spiritual insight is married to intellectual ability, and coupled with a delight in the use of the intellect. This Sutra, it is true, points to something that lies far beyond the intellect. But the way to get to That is to follow the intellect as far as it will take you. And the dialectical logic of this Sutra enables the intellect, working through language, to carry the understanding a stage further than the conceptual thinking based on ordinary logic can do.

Tradition assumed that three kinds of persons could win enlightenment, i.e. Arhats, Pratyekabuddhas and Buddhas. The enlightenment of a Buddha is more complete than that of the others, and 'omniscience' is its distinguishing feature. No. 48 gives the technical term reserved for it. It is **utmost** because no one can go higher on the way of self-abandonment. It is **right** because it is not 'wrong' (see no. 57). It is **perfect** in the sense of being complete.

Here ends the metaphysical part, and with it the main body

of the Sutra. I must now redeem my promise to show how it
constitutes a re-statement of the four holy Truths. The first
sermon of the Buddha, which at Benares proclaimed the four
holy Truths, is called the 'Sutra by which the Wheel of Dharma
has been set rolling' (*dharma-cakra-pravartana-sūtra*). The
Prajñāpāramitā Scriptures, of which the *Hridaya* is an abbrevia-
tion, maintain that this was only a provisional, relatively
primitive, teaching. The Prajñāpāramitā doctrine represents
the 'second turning of the Wheel of the Dharma'.[1] It brings out
the deeper meaning of the original doctrine, which is re-inter-
preted in the light of the dominant idea of Emptiness. This must
involve also the four holy Truths, and the Heart Sutra is
designed as the *dharmacakrapravartana-sūtra* of the new dis-
pensation. Some years ago I gave a detailed proof of this thesis
in the *Journal of the Royal Asiatic Society* (1948, pp. 33–51), and
I am now content to show how it works out for each one of the
four Truths. Readers who do not know the Sermon of Benares
by heart will do well to refresh their memory by looking up its
exact formulation (e.g. *B* p. 43). Section II of the *Hridaya*
corresponds to the first Truth, III to the second, IV and V to the
third, and VI and VII to the fourth. As follows:

I. The traditional formula equated '*ill*' with the 'five
grasping skandhas'. In section II we heard that Avalokiteśvara,
when he compassionately surveys the sufferings of beings, sees
just the skandhas, and that these in their turn are emptiness.
The fact of ill seems at first sight to presuppose the existence
of suffering creatures. With increasing wisdom these 'beings'
are seen as groups, or heaps, of skandhas. Finally, with perfect
wisdom, the skandhas turn out to be Emptiness, and compassion
proceeds with no object at all (see *BT* no. 168). In actual
reality, the fact of ill cannot maintain itself against the fact of
emptiness.

II. The traditional formula attributed the *origination* of ill to
craving. This craving, the cause of ill, is bound up with the
skandhas, and found in them. In section III these skandhas are
pronounced to be identical with emptiness, and not separate
from it. They have never left the original Void, and so in reality
they have never originated.

III. The third Truth in its original form stated that the

[1] *The Perfection of Wisdom in 8,000 Lines*, chapter IX, p. 203.

stopping of craving leads to the *stopping* of ill. In sections IV and V this is held to mean that the 'stopping' of which the Scriptures have spoken is really an 'emptiness' which is devoid of any dharma. In this emptiness there can be no stopping, because one cannot speak of something as stopped if it never existed, or came into being, or originated.

IV. The Sermon of Benares had enumerated the eight 'limbs', or constituents, of the *Path* which leads to the cessation of ill. In the *Prajñāpāramitā* literature, interest has moved altogether away from them, and has shifted to the last stages of a Bodhisattva's career. Section VI deals with the achievements of the last three of the ten stages of a Bodhisattva, and Section VII with the stage of a Buddha.

These brief remarks must here suffice. The *Prajñāpāramitā* texts are so elusive to our understanding not only because they presuppose a high degree of disinterested spirituality, but also because they are full of hidden hints, allusions and indirect references to the pre-existing body of scriptures and traditions, which circulated in the memory of the Buddhist community at the time when they were composed. They are more often than not an echo of older sayings. Without the relation to them they lose most of their point. We at present must reconstruct laboriously what 1,500 years ago seemed a matter of course.

VIII. THE TEACHING BROUGHT WITHIN THE REACH OF
THE COMPARATIVELY UNENLIGHTENED

Tasmāj jñātavyam: prajñāpāramitā mahā-mantro mahā-vidyā-mantro 'nuttara-mantro' samasama-mantraḥ, sarva-duḥkha-praśamanaḥ, satyam amithyatvāt. prajñāpāramitāyām ukto mantraḥ. tadyathā: gate gate pāragate pārasaṃgate bodhi svāhā. iti prajñāpāramitā-hridayaṃ samāptam.

[50]Therefore one should know [51]the prajñāpāramitā [52]as the great spell, [53]the spell of great knowledge, [54]the utmost spell, [55]the unequalled spell, [56]allayer of all suffering, [57]in truth—for what could go wrong? [58]By the prajñāpāramitā has this spell been delivered. [59]It runs like this: [60]Gone, gone, gone beyond, gone altogether beyond,

O what an awakening, all-hail!—⁶¹This completes the Heart of perfect wisdom.

The explanation of the individual terms must here again, as in section V, be preceded by a survey of the progress of the argument. Four main subdivisions can be distinguished:

1. (*a*) Because you are potentially a Buddha yourself (this refers back to section VII), (*b*) and because Avalokiteśvara in his mercy would not allow you to perish or despair (this refers back to section II), (*c*) he will find a way to bridge the gap between your present state on the one hand, and the practice of transcendental wisdom, as outlined in nos. 10–49, on the other. (*d*) Avalokiteśvara, known traditionally as the 'bestower of spells' (*vidyā-adhipati*), has therefore given us a wonder-working mantra in which the perfection of wisdom is condensed.

2. This mantra (*a*) has the traditional attributes of a Buddha (nos. 52–5; refer back to nos. 45–9), (*b*) is likened to Nirvana (nos. 56–7; refer back to no. 44), and (*c*) derives its power from transcendental wisdom (no. 58).

3. It either helps you to (*a*) identify yourself with transcendental wisdom as a force latent in, and yet external to you (*gate* as a feminine vocative), or (*b*) to define emptiness in relation to your present state by indicating the steps which you must take to get to it (*gate* as a masculine or feminine locative) (no. 60).

4. Here, in this Sutra, or mantra, you have the very heart of transcendental wisdom (no. 61).

The meaning of **therefore** has been supplied in 1 (*a*)–(*d*) above. **A spell** (*mantra*) is a magical incantation, or formula. Such a mantra, it must be admitted, is certainly more tangible than pure Emptiness, and more eloquent than the speechlessness of the highest possible enlightenment. **The Prajñāpāramitā,** in other contexts a book, a deity, an image, or a spiritual perfection, is here envisaged as a spell.

Mantras are incantations which effect wonders when uttered. According to the *Sādhanamālā* there is nothing that they cannot achieve, if applied according to the rules. But the rules are, of course, hard to come by. Some mantras give miraculous protection in adversity, and my great predecessor Hsüan-tsang used the *Hridaya* in this manner when in the Gobi desert 'he encountered all sorts of demon shapes and strange goblins'. 'When he recited this Sutra, at the sound of the words they all disappeared in a moment. Whenever he was in danger, it was to this alone that he trusted for his safety and deliverance'.

Generally, however, personal safety is entrusted to other mantras. The wondrous effect of the *Hridaya* mantra lies in that it opens the mind to enlightenment.

It is, on the other hand, not the fault of mantras that in this present age they run up against the general incomprehension of magical forces which the vulgarization of science has fostered among town-dwellers. A mantra is efficacious because it enshrines a spiritual principle, or, in mythological terms, because it establishes a relation between its user and a deity, in this case the Prajñāpāramitā. Transcendental wisdom has her being in a mantra, and can thus be apprehended by its repetition and manifold practice. According to the magical theory, mantras should be sung, chanted, spoken, murmured, mumbled or whispered. The exact sound-value of each Sanskrit syllable is then important and must carefully be attended to.[1] Alternatively, intent gazing (*vipaśyanā*) on its written letters, placed on an eight-petalled lotus, is recommended (see the Illustration).[2] Whichever method may be adopted, the constant presence of the mantra in the mind should be aimed at. As we read in the *Yoga Sutras* (II 44): 'From repetition of the mantra comes communion with the intended deity'. The *Hridaya* mantra is a means of courting or wooing the Perfection of Wisdom. As it is said in the *Wisdom of Solomon* (VI 12): 'Wisdom is glorious and never fadeth away. Yes, she is easily seen of them that love her, and found of such as seek her.'

Knowledge, *vidyā*, has here the meaning of magical 'lore'. The word connects the mantra with the Buddha, for 'perfect in knowledge and conduct' is the fourth of the ten standard epithets of a Buddha (see *BM* p. 46). **Utmost** means 'supreme', it is the sixth of the Buddha's epithets, and we met it before (at no. 48) as one of the distinctive features of the Buddha's enlightenment. **Unequalled,** more literally 'equal to the unequalled', is also a traditional attribute of the Buddhas. It means 'incomparable', or it is that which makes one equal that which cannot be equalled.

In nos. 56-7 the mantra is then equated with Nirvana, which is traditionally known as the **allayer of all suffering.** In addition this spell is contrasted with other mantras, which are normally adapted to removing a specific evil, illness, or threat. This spell on the other hand, because it aims at enlightenment itself, is designed to remove *all* evil. And is it not true that complete renunciation must automatically get rid of all ills? **In truth**—the word *satyam* comes from the root *as* 'to be',

[1] The reader should remember that in Sanskrit the vowel *e* is always long. The short *a* is pronounced as in b*u*t, the long *ā* as in father, ask, etc., the *e* as in m*a*te, l*a*me, etc. The metrical scheme of the mantra is as follows: gaté gaté páragaté párasámgate bódhi svahá.

[2] In the centre, to correspond to the seed vessel, I have placed the syllable *Oṃ*. Sometimes, as in *Oṃ maṇi padme hūṃ*, the *oṃ* is an essential part of the mantra. Here, however, it is an optional and extraneous addition, and only a minority of the manuscripts, and generally the later ones, contain it. The Brahmins regard the *Oṃ* as the source of all the other letters, and *Bhagavadgita* xvii 24 informs us that 'acts of sacrifice, etc., enjoined in the scriptures, are always *begun* with an *Oṃ* by the students of Brahma'.

and corresponds etymologically to 'sooth' in English. It can here be either an adverb or a noun. In the translation I have taken it as an adverb, which refers back to no. 56, and asserts that this mantra 'indeed truly' removes all ill, because it is not wrongness, i.e. without any trace whatsoever of division. Alternatively, we may understand that it, i.e. the mantra, is 'the Truth'. 'Truth' is a synonym for Nirvana, and Buddhaghosa (VM 497) tells us that the saying of Suttanipāta 884, 'For one single is the Truth, and there is no second', refers to Nirvana, which exists in the ultimate sense.

'Truth' should then here be understood as the One in contrast to the manifold variety of error, as that which is just so, just itself, Suchness. It is taken as just Truth, Truth by itself, Truth absolute, nothing but the Truth, simple and really existing Truth, by contrast to the falsehood and illusion of imaginary duplicity, duality, multiplicity. Its essence is agreement, sameness, identity—not agreement of a proposition with a thing, or of a thing with the conception we may form of it, but agreement of itself alone with Itself alone, of emptiness, of nothing in particular, with itself. To miss that is 'wrongness'.

Nirvana, and this mantra, is the Truth—a-mithyatvād, literally, 'because there is no wrongness' in it. The word comes from the root mith, which recurs in English in the prefix mis-, and in the verb 'to miss', and carries with it the suggestion of duality and conflict. Where the Absolute is alone, unassociated, aloof from all, what could go wrong, in the absence of all duality and thereby of all possibility of deviating from the Truth? Wrong and perverted views, the supreme fault, consist in straying away from supreme Oneness, which as the Truth is also the Way.

By the Prajñāpāramitā has this spell been delivered. 'Prajñāpāramitā' is here Wisdom personified. Mantras are more than just well-sounding words cunningly arranged by ingenious persons. According to tradition they are gifts from higher beings, through which they communicate a part of their essential nature. You do not really know where you are with a spell before you know where it comes from, and who gave it its power. The word ukta more literally would mean, 'spoken, uttered, taught, or proclaimed', but the meaning of the phrase cannot be that this spell has been proclaimed in the *Prajñāpāramitā* books. Nowhere do the large *Prajñāpāramitā Sutras* contain this particular, or any other, mantra.

Gone—the ending *-e* in *gate*, etc., can, grammatically, have two meanings: (1) It may denote a feminine vocative—'O, she (i.e. the Prajñāpāramitā), who is gone, etc.!' The mantra would then resume the initial invocation (no. 1). Or, (2) it may be a masculine locative—'In him who is gone, etc., there is enlightenment'. Then it states, as I have shown in some detail in *SS* pp. 22–4, what must be done to get to enlightenment. The locative can in Sanskrit be used as an absolute case, and the meaning then would be; 'he is gone' etc. The mantra therefore represents a dialogue with an invisible force, or with oneself.

Beyond, *pāra,* occurs, as we saw at no. 5, in the very name of the *prajñā-pāram-itā.* As a technical term it is opposed to a Not-Beyond, which comprises: (1) suffering, (2) its basis, i.e. the round of births, (3) the place where suffering takes place, i.e. the skandhas, and (4) its cause, i.e. craving and other bad habits. The unwholesome states are compared to a flood, or to a river in full spate. We are on the hither shore, beset with fears and dangers. Security can be found only on the other shore, beyond the flood, which has to be crossed by means of the ship, or raft, of the Dharma.

Awakening, equals enlightenment (of no. 48), wisdom, emptiness and Nirvana (no. 44).

All hail, *svāhā,* only imperfectly reproduced by 'all hail', is a term of blessing used traditionally by the Brahmin priests in their ritual. It is an ecstatic shout of joy, expressive of a feeling of complete release, just as *Io triumpe* was in Latin, *Hailly* in Mexican, or *Axie taure* in Dionysian ritual. In the Tantric system *svāhā* is reserved for mantras addressed to feminine deities.

The six words of the mantra correspond to sections III to VIII respectively. This is quite obvious for *bodhi,* which takes up the 'enlightenment' of section VII. After the two initial steps of sections III and IV we come to V at the *pāragate*, which is the traditional term for the plunge into the Unconditioned. In *pāra-saṃ-gate*, the *saṃ-* has the meaning of completeness, as with *saṃ-bodhi* in no. 48. Readers can work out the further details for themselves.

LIST OF ABBREVIATIONS

A = *Aṣṭasāhasrikā prajñāpāramitā-sūtra*, ed. R. Mitra, 1888.
B = *Buddhism. Its essence and development*, by Edward Conze, 3rd ed., 1957.
BM = *Buddhist Meditation*, by Edward Conze, 1956.
BT = *Buddhist Texts through the Ages*, ed. E. Conze, 1954.
Mpps = *Mahāprajñāpāramitopadeśa*, by Nāgārjuna, trans. E. Lamotte, as *Le traité de la grande vertue de sagesse*, I 1944, II 1949.
P = *Pañcaviṃśatisāhasrikā prajñāpāramitā-sūtra*, ed. N. Dutt, 1934.
SS = *Selected Sayings from the Perfection of Wisdom*, ed. E. Conze, 1955.
T = *Taishō Issaikyō*.
VM = *Visuddhimagga*, by Buddhaghosa, ed. C. A. F. Rhys Davids, 1920–21.

INDEX OF TERMS

Abhidharma, 81
Absolute, 39
Ānanda, 21
anuttara, 61, 98, 104
anxiety, 97
araṇā, 45
Arhat, 45, 93, 99
ārya, 38, 77
ātmabhāva, 49
atoms, 64–5
attainment, 92, 97–8
avācya, 37, 66
Avalokiteśvara, 78, 102
āvaraṇa, 67, 95

being, 33, 54, 100
Beyond, 78, 106
Bhagavatī, 77
Bodhisattva, 23, 78, 94
Buddha, 98–9
Buddhadharmas, 42, 58
Buddhafield, 46–7

caitya, 50
citta, 25, 95
cognition, 53, 92, 99
consciousness, 63, 82
create, 47

dharma, 44, 81, 85–6
Dharmabody, 29–30, 42, 48, 63
dialectics, 52, 84–5
Diamond Sutra, 10, 51
Dipankara, 46, 56, 58
dwells, 95

emptiness, 65, 80–1, 83, 86
enlightenment, 48, 98–9
eyes (five): 59

faith, 29, 32
feelings, 82
foolish common people, 62, 66
form, 25, 82
forms, 55, 91
fraud, 29, 55, 58

gnosis, 92

Heart Sutra, 10
holy, 38, 77
Holy Persons, 38

ignorance, 68–9
impulses, 82
īśvara, 78

Jeta Grove, 22

karmaresult, 57
kulaputra, 24

mahāsattva, 23
mantra, 19–20, 101–7
marks (3): 86, 97
marks (32): 28–9, 52, 60, 62–3
merit, 27–8, 33, 41, 55, 62
mind-objects, 91

nairātmya (twofold): 34, 87–8
Never-returner, 44
Nirvana, 26, 47, 82–3, 97, 104–5
nishpādayati, 47

Once-returner, 44
own-being, 80

pāramitā, 53
patience, 54, 63
Peace, 45
perceptions, 82
perfect, 99
person, 33
perverted views, 97, 105
piṇḍa, 65–6
prabhāvita, 39
prajñāpāramitā, 48, 52, 62, 78, 98,
102, 106
precious things (7) 40, 63
pṛthak, 81, 88

raft, 35
right, 99

sampad, 28
Śāriputra, 45, 81
satya, 104–5
self, 33
shrine, 50, 56
sign, 27, 68
skandha, 41, 79, 82, 84, 100
soul, 33
spell, 101–4
Śrāvastī, 22
states of woe, 56
Streamwinner, 44
Subhūti, 45
Suchness, 37, 58, 68, 96
Sumeru, 49, 62
śūnyatā, 19, 80–1
superknowledge, 54, 56, 59
svāhā, 106